Screwed Up Somehow but Not Stupid

Screwed Up Somehow but Not Stupid

life with a learning diability

Peter Flom, Ph.D.

IAmLearningDisabled.com

Design by Indigo Editing & Publications.

Printed in the United States of America.

ISBN: 978-0-692-61169-2

To the memory of Elizabeth Friedus

Contents

Preface

You may be thinking, "What kind of title is that?"

"What is a phrase like 'screwed up' doing in a title?"

"And what about the word 'stupid' (even with a "not" before it)?" That's no way to talk about other people, right?

Well, I'm not talking about "other" people. I'm talking about myself and others like me. There is something distinctly different about the way my mind works. It took me a long time to get comfortable expressing it, but it's real. I have a nonverbal learning disability (NLD or NLVD, for short). Maybe you do, too. Or maybe your child has NLD or a friend, or maybe you're a teacher and you wonder whether some kids in your class have NLD. Or maybe you're just interested. Welcome.

Life is different for a person with NLD. We NLDers often appear "odd." We have trouble making friends. Our weird areas of disability don't match the stereotype of the phrase learning disability. We NLDers are not stupid, we're not lazy (or no more so than the average person), but we are screwed up somehow. We'll never be completely "normal" or "neuro-typical" (NT, the acronym for people who think they don't need one). But we *can* enjoy improved lives. We can have hope, help, and happiness. This book explores how we NLDers can help ourselves and how we can help you NT folks help us, which in turn helps us all.

This book is for anyone who is interested in NLD, but I've added sections in this preface for certain groups:

- Young people with NLD
- Adults with NLD
- Teachers
- Parents

FOR YOUNG PEOPLE WITH NLD

For many people with NLD, the years between 12 and 18 are the most difficult. This is a hard age for many NT people, but it's an especially hard age to be different, to stand out from the crowd. Many adolescents want to conform, to be part of the "in" crowd.

Keep in mind is that other people at this age are also different. They're just differently different. Some people who seem like the most popular are, secretly, also different. Part of the problem of being NLD is that our disability is not obvious; we act differently because we think differently. It's not clear to others why we have difficulties. Contrast this with someone who is blind or wheelchair-bound. Their problems are more disabling, but also more visibly obvious.

I am not going to tell NLDers that you're just like other kids your age; you're not. But I'll try to make it a little easier to be different. And, if your parents are reading this book, I'll try to impart some of what I've learned.

FOR ADULTS WITH NLD

In some ways, today's non-verbal learning disabled adults have it harder than the kids coming after us: Back when we were kids, little was known how people learn or about learning disabilities (LD), much less NLD. When I was a kid, the term learning disabled was known about by only a few people. Resources were scarce; books were nonexistent; support groups were few and far between. Now we've learned a lot about NLD. I hope that some of what I say in this book will prove useful, add to your coping strategies, and give you an easier life.

One of the challenges for many NLDers is the shift from school to work, and I have much to say about this in Chapter 11. Another troublesome area is relationships, also discussed in Chapter 11. Almost all of the NLD adults I know have significant difficulties with various areas of life, but they can also have very good lives. Many adult NLDers have fulfilling relationships and good jobs, defining success on their own terms so that they realize they are successful in the ways that matter to them, regardless of whether they are successful as is usually defined in America today.

FOR TEACHERS

First, let me say that I think the vast majority of teachers are doing as good a job as they can, and are overworked, underpaid, and burdened with all sorts of stuff with no direct connection to education.

Two sorts of teachers may be interested in what I have to say: 1) Special education teachers who want to learn about an LD mentioned infrequently, even in special education literature, but who teach some students who don't fit any of the more well-known diagnoses; and 2) teachers of general education who have one or two NLD kids in their classes. Chapters 8 to 10 may be of interest to both groups.

FOR PARENTS

Parents want to know all they can about their children, whether the difficulties that arise prior to school or at school. They may be overwhelmed by technical jargon, competing diagnoses, labels that don't seem to fit, and so on. Also, their child can easily be given a diagnosis that does not fit as well as NLD.

You'll find encouragement and help throughout the book. Chapter 6 has coping mechanisms for parents for kids of every age, and Chapter 7 is specific to the NLD child at home. There is hope.

1: Who Is Peter?

PETER IS SCREWED UP IN SOME WAY...BUT NOT STUPID.

I am, as I write this, 55 years old. I have NLD (nonverbal learning disabilities), or something like it. I've never been formally diagnosed with NLD, but this diagnosis fits me best.

It became clear that something was wrong in my early childhood. Even the preschool director asked me not to return. At age 5, a psychologist informed my parents I would never attend college. In reaction to this news, my mother met with her friend Elizabeth Friedus and started a school for me—The Gateway School of New York. It still exists.

I left Gateway at age 9 to attend the Emerson School (now closed). Then, in sixth grade, I moved on to York Preparatory School. Both Emerson and York were more-or-less mainstream schools. York has a large number of children with learning issues but theirs are mostly the opposite of mine. Many York students have academic problems and are socially adept. I had no academic problems, but was a mess socially. (More on this later.)

Then, despite the psychologist's prediction, I not only attended college (New York University) but also skipped my senior year of high school and completed college in 3 ½ years, graduating at age 20. Later, I earned a Master's degree in special education and a Ph.D. in psychometrics. I'm married and have two sons. I work as a freelance statistician and as a consultant about NLD.

CHILDHOOD: YUP, HE'S WEIRD

My earliest memory is an isolated one: bouncing on my cot at preschool. I don't remember much else until I attended Gateway, the school my mother opened for children with disabilities. Gateway was and is a wonderfully accepting place. When Gateway opened its doors, three students enrolled. By the time I graduated (and for a long time thereafter) it had about 30. Now, in a new building and serving children from age 5 through eighth grade, it has well over 100 students. My first teacher at Gateway was Grace Kumar, who I remember telling us "be gentle, that's a human being" when we got rough on each other.

At about age 9, nearing the end of my Gateway years, I took an IQ test (the WISC). Like most intelligence tests, it had subtests. Most people receive similar scores on the subtests. I did not. My subtest scores ranged from 60 to 160. The wide range of scores suggests a learning disability; the way I perceive things vastly differs from a neuro-typical (NT) person. My lowest scores were on "performance" tests, especially spatial perception. My best scores were on "information" and "vocabulary." The scores appropriately identified how I function. I have difficulty with spatial relationships to this day while I easily work in academia and data-driven tasks and projects.

In fifth grade my math teacher was "old school" and thought that a child who failed to complete multiplication problems was unprepared for division. I was never able to learn my times tables the usual way kids learn them; I later made up tricks. (I share my tricks in Chapter 8.) My messy handwriting made things worse; the teacher tried to decipher my numerals but couldn't, and marked many correct problems "wrong." She assigned me to remedial math over the summer. But since I excel at math, my tutor taught me several years of math that summer.

Truly a learning disability is a question of how people learn best and how they can express their intelligence. My "remedial math" summer showed I learned well in an environment that acknowledged and supported my disability. Learning modalities matter.

What was my ideal summer away from school? A big pile of books in my room from which I'd emerge for meals only. I liked to read the almanac. I liked music written long before I was born. Sports? Forget it.

I was a strange kid.

ADOLESCENCE: THE NADIR OF EXISTENCE

Adolescence is a messy stage of life for most people. For me, this messy stage was the nadir of existence. The good news? Each year after age 15 has been at least as good, and usually better, than the one before. The bad news? Around age 15 life sucked!

My parents enrolled me in York Prep in sixth grade, a poor choice for me. Choosing a school for a learning disabled child (whether NLD or another LD) requires an academic *and* social fit. Academically astute, I averaged only fifteen minutes a night of homework, much less than the teachers intended.

I was bored in class and obnoxious to many of my teachers. For example, I told a teacher that I did not have to listen to her because she was not as smart as I was. However, I had some good teachers at York. I remember fondly Malcolm Spaull, who taught Math (see below) Dominic Michel, who taught English, and Helen Lambeth, who taught Social Studies.

In sixth grade, Malcolm Spaull taught me math. On the first night, I took the book home and read it. (Yeah, I read the math book). The next day I told Mr. Spaull that it was easy. He said it got harder. I said I had done the whole book. He quizzed me on sixth, seventh, and eighth grade math and then switched me to his ninth grade class. Like I said, no academic problem!

But I continued to make insensitive remarks to teachers and other students, like "This is easy. Why don't you understand it?" I was clueless! A social mess!

COLLEGE: THINGS GET BETTER

In 1977 I became a student at New York University. For me and many NLDers, life improves in college for several reasons. First, maturity. Not only was I more mature, so were my age mates. At York Prep, kids tended to act the same way with the same people. No miracle happens over the summer between high school and college; your peers change. I hung out with other young adults, I no longer hung out with adolescents. Second, in college, there are more choices of activities and friends. In high school, you attend classes with the same people, and after school you have homework, and a limited range of activities (at least at a small school). In college you spend less time in class and have more freedom to structure your time. You also have a wider range of classes to choose from and many more people to hang with (I went from a high school with about 150 students to a university with 40,000), clubs to go to, places to be, and so on.

I did well at a large university; some NLDers learn better in smaller colleges. A distinguishing mark of large schools is "slipping between the cracks." For me, this was a good thing. I needed to slip through some cracks. I needed to be in a place where no one knew me, where I could be anonymous. In high school, everyone knew me. They all knew I was weird and made fun of me.

In college, if I did something dorky in one environment, no one knew in other environments because each class and club had different people. Plus, with thousands of students at NYU, I didn't stick out. Plenty of other students were somewhat like me. To be the "odd one" in a small school does not require much "oddness." To stand out at a large university, you really have to be something unusual! In fact, it's safe to say that there was no "oddest" student at NYU—because there are so many ways to be odd.

While adolescents typically value conformity, young adults often value uniqueness. Adolescence is about fitting in and discovering who you are and which group you belong in. One way of defining the group you belong in is to decide who to exclude. I got to be the excluded one from a lot of high school groups—I didn't fit in any typical niche. In young adulthood, many people want to stand out. They know what group they belong to and they are eager to show that they are unique. This is an appealing social task for a person like me.

ADULTHOOD: EVEN BETTER

Adulthood is much easier than childhood and adolescence—especially adolescence. As I mentioned my nadir of existence was age 15. Year by year, life improved and plateaued from age 30 to now, with, of course, some ups and downs along the way. Again, adults have more control over their lives. Who tells you whom to hang out with? *You do.* Who tells you what to do with your free time? *You do.* Who tells you when to go to bed? *You do.* And so on. This is especially true if you can manage your work environment. Unfortunately, a lot of adults with NLD are unemployed or underemployed. Fortunately for me, I thrived in my work environment. (More on navigating the workplace in Chapter 11.)

Also, by adulthood, I had at least somewhat figured out who I was, although my career didn't get settled until relatively late–I first started working with data in my early 30s–and I didn't marry until later in life as well. Now, at 55, both of those landmarks seem long ago!

FIVE MISTAKES PEOPLE MAKE WHEN DEALING WITH NLDERS
When a person with NLD interacts with a neuro-typical person,
things can go wrong. No list can prevent all the ways it can go
wrong, but here are some mistakes NT people make when interacting with us NLDers:

1. *Assuming we're stupid.* Often a person with NLD won't
   "get" something that the NT person is saying. It's a sort
   of natural reaction on the NT person's part to assume
   that the person who doesn't "get" things is cognitively
   limited, or, in blunt terms, stupid. It's true that stupid
   people often fail to get things; but there can be other
   reasons: we NLDers don't process information the same
   way most people do.

2. *Assuming we're deaf.* This seems a common mistake when
   dealing with anyone with a disability. Friends of mine
   who use wheelchairs say people yell at them all the time,
   as if the problems with their legs related to problems
   with their ears. Most people with NLD hear perfectly
   well. Some of us, however, have trouble when there are
   multiple conversations going on at once. (I know I do.)
   We also tend to miss the nonverbal aspects of language–
   body language, facial expression, tone of voice, and so on.

3. *Assuming we're not listening.* Since NLD people have trouble processing nonverbal information, we may look away
   more often than most people do. Sometimes information
   from multiple stimuli can overwhelm us. I listen better
   when I am not paying attention to a person's face.

4. *Assuming we're not interested in you.* OK, sometimes we
   really aren't interested in you! Just like sometimes other
   NT people aren't interested in you. But NT people use
   small talk and social chitchat to judge interest, and many

NLD people just don't get chitchat. We are often much better when the conversation moves to substantive topics.

5. *Assuming we're like other "spectrum" people you know.* There's a lot of talk about an "autism spectrum," and many people think NLD is on it. Whether we are or not, we're each individuals. **When you've seen one person with NLD, you've seen one person with NLD.**

LABELS ARE USEFUL, BUT BOXES ARE FOR GROCERIES

The special education world is chock full of labels. Sometimes these labels are used strictly for funding purposes. The labels are often drawn directly out of the latest DSM (Diagnostic and Statistical Manual of Mental Disorders) and correspond to some diagnosis listed there. But other labels are used to help people (parents, teachers, administrators and—oh my!—even the person with the label) understand what is going on, find resources, and locate people with similar issues. Of course, people are complex and labels are simple. So it's not the "right" label to aim for, but the "best fitting" label.

Take me, for example (the example I know best!). My best-fitting label is NLD. Is this label "right"? Well … people with NLD are not supposed to have any sense of humor! (Where do I go to return mine?) Also, we're not supposed to be good at math. I am, no kidding, a statistician! So maybe the label isn't right. But it's a better fit than any other label I've come across.

That's because the key aspect of NLD is that we are not good at nonverbal stuff. And I am not good at nonverbal stuff. It's also because, when I discuss my issues with other NLDers, they often say things like, "Yeah, me too!"—and I often say that to them. While I have some characteristics of autism and Asperger's and dyspraxia and who knows what else, those labels don't fit as well as NLD.

So, when you (or your child or your student) is labeled, don't expect to get the right label—there may not be one, but try to use the best-fitting label. Labels describe people, they don't define them.

Some people in the world of LD dislike labels. I don't fully share that dislike. I think what they are objecting to is the *abuse* of labels, and certainly that abuse is prevalent. But labels can be very useful. Labels can help us get help; they can help us realize we aren't alone; they can help us get funding. The problem is that sometimes we let a label become a box into which we must fit—and people don't fit well into boxes.

I am a husband, a father, a liberal, a statistician, and a New Yorker. Each describes me but, even in total, they don't define me. Labels for learning disabilities can be helpful much as labeling other things is helpful. For example, if a doctor labels a patient has having a certain disease, it can point the way toward finding a specialist, making a prognosis, and determining treatment. At the same time, doctors should be aware that each patient is different. Similarly with learning disabilities: It can help us figure things out.

Like I said, labels describe me, but they don't define me. And labels don't define you or your child either.

2: What Is NLD? Part 1

By definition, a nonverbal learning disability (NLD) is a kind of learning disability, or LD, in which nonverbal communication is a huge problem. Many years ago experts treated LD as a single disorder, believing all LD individuals have much in common. This led to research comparing learning-disabled people to matched controls who were not LD. It was also marked by a very narrow idea of what types of deficits could be called LD. This approach is inadequate because LDs are marked more by their differences than their similarities.

With hindsight, it is obvious that people who have significant difficulties with mathematics (dyscalculia) differ from those with significant difficulties with reading (dyslexia). However, early in the history of LD research, dyslexia was seen as almost synonymous with LD as a whole. For a non-expert, it is still easy to get that view today—a lot of the literature on LD focuses on dyslexia.

The technical term for this sort of view is *nomothetic*. In reaction to it, some adapted an *idiographic* approach, in which every LD individual is seen as entirely unique, to the extent that generalizations about groups of LD individuals are virtually or entirely impossible. While this approach has more appeal to me than the nomothetic one, it is nevertheless clear that some groups of individuals share much in common.

The question then becomes what these groups are, and what they share in common. It is also important to remember that, despite the existence of similarities among groups of people, each individual is unique, with characteristics that may cross different groups as traditionally defined.

In the late 1980s, research began to take a more sensible, less extreme position, recognizing that both the idiographic and nomothetic approaches are too limited. In addition, research began to be based on theoretical models of learning disabilities, rather than on purely empirical investigations or on very general theories of learning. Although each individual (learning disabled or not) is unique, LD people can be grouped in various ways, including ways based on shared strengths and weaknesses.

In the vernacular, I like to say that labels can be useful, but boxes are for groceries. . In other traits, we recognize this without any problem: None of us would think that all tall people are alike, yet we all recognize that some people are tall.

A traditional view of LD holds that it's a type of learning problem *not* due to emotional problems, mental retardation, sensory handicap, poor instruction, poor motivation, or cultural or linguistic deprivation (Rourke, 1995). Stewart (2005) notes that an LD is "an inability to learn material and to perform or produce work at a level equal to your potential or intelligence." Mamen (2007) reports that LDs may impair the "acquisition, organization, retention, understanding or use of verbal or nonverbal information." (In the next chapter, we consider these definitions in depth.)

THE MYKLEBUST BREAKTHROUGH

Homer R. Myklebust coined the "nonverbal learning disabilities" in 1975. Myklebust noted that, while researchers had done little work nonverbal *disabilities*, including terminology, the *importance* of nonverbal skills had long been recognized, and had been included on many tests that purport to measure intelligence, including the first ones, developed by French psychologist Alfred Binet in the late 1800s. It is interesting to note that the terminology Myklebust used—phrases such as time agnosia, anosognosia and asterognosis—have fallen out of favor. However, much of what Myklebust said remains relevant today.

He recognized that there are various types of nonverbal disabilities and noted that treatment should be specific to the particular type of diagnosis. He decried the lack of ability to correctly classify children into these smaller groups—which is only beginning to be addressed, 40 years later. He also noted patterns of score on the WISC that are similar to those found today. NLD children did particularly poorly on block design, picture completion, picture arrangement, coding and mazes (on a personal note, these are *exactly* the subtests that I did worst on). He presented several case studies. Finally, and perhaps most important, he noted that "those who have marked involvement are the ones seen most often; those who have mild to moderate involvement go unrecognized, compensating for their disability as best they can."

So, what is an NLD, generally? How can a person be learning disabled and yet read well and perhaps excel in math? Let's answer these questions briefly before going into them more deeply.

What is an NLD, generally? An NLD is a neurological impairment affecting a person's abilities in many areas but typically ones not related to speech. Common areas of difficulty are reading body language, reading faces, discerning tone of voice, being aware of one's own body, face, and tone of voice, remembering faces, correctly estimating the amount of time to complete a task, having good temporal or spatial memory, trouble with math and visual skills, and poor coordination and spatial perception.

How can someone have an LD yet read well or excel in math? Anything an adult knows had to be learned. Babies are born with few skills: sucking, urinating, crying, and a few other things. Everything else is learned. These skills tend to go together in various ways. If you are much worse at one set of these skills than at most others, the disparity suggests an LD. Most people think an LD relates only to what you learn in school—and it certainly **can** involve reading (dyslexia), math (dyscalculia), and other school skills. But most NLDers are academically astute while socially inept. Yes, you can have an LD and be gifted. Why not? You can be tall and fat, or skinny and short, can't you?

A MISUNDERSTANDING OF NLD

As I've stated, many people think that an LD must be about academic difficulties, primarily with reading or math. Educators and parents are aware of other conditions that affect learning, like attention deficit hyperactivity disorder (ADHD). If you wander in the "children with special needs" section of a large bookstore, you will see many books on dyslexia, ADHD, autism-spectrum disorders, and Asperger's syndrome (AS). You will be lucky to find even one book on NLD. One way to compare the coverage of different LDs is to look at Google. I recently did this (May 2014): "nonverbal learning disability," 312,000 hits; ADHD, 16 *million*; dyslexia, 3 *million*; autism, a whopping 20 *million*.

If you tell people that you are LD but never had problems in school (at least, not with the academics), then they either don't understand or don't believe you, thinking you are making excuses and are lazy, crazy or stupid. This is nonsensical. If the LD doesn't happen to involve academics, then it doesn't involve academics. Everyone (including the people making those comments) knows that there is much more to life than book learning.

NLDers struggle with other important skills not taught in school: reading body language, correctly estimating the amount of time to complete a task, having good temporal or spatial memory, and much else.

NLDers are, in a way, the opposite of animals. Your pet dog hears your tone of voice and the feel of your touch and understands what you're communicating; your actual words don't matter. NLDers get your words. But your tone, your expression, even your touch—we don't understand their meaning.

Another defining characteristic of NLD is problems with sensory integration. Sensory integration is the process of understanding the information that assaults our senses each minute. NLDers may be over- or under-sensitive to stimuli (Whitney 2002). Also, they may be oversensitive to stimuli in one area and under-sensitive in another; they may find any noise objectionable but be fine with extremes of temperature. Or they may find certain textures objectionable (either in clothing or food) but accept other textures.

STRANGERS IN OUR OWN LAND

Neuro-typical people who deal with NLDers would like to understand us. Misunderstanding is very frustrating to both the NLDer and other people. Here, I share an analogy and hints of what it is like to be me: We feel like strangers in our own land. What do I mean by this? If you (and by "you" I mean an interested NTer) have ever been to a foreign country, particularly one with a culture very different from your own , then you probably ran into problems. The natives were doing weird things! They acted in odd ways! They got upset with you for "normal" behavior!

There are many ways in which culture influences our behavior. If you were in a country where you didn't look like a native, then the natives may not have expected you to speak their language.

They may have attempted to speak English. But that's the *verbal* part. Nonverbal communication matters too.

Gestures that mean one thing in one country may mean something very different in another. For example, a gesture that means "wait a minute" in Israel means something rude in Italy and in some American cultures. Nonverbal communication includes personal space too. The people in that foreign country may have stood too close to you or touched you too often for your comfort. Americans, especially Americans of northern and western European descent, tend to be on the low end of "touch"—other cultures touch much more. Their facial expressions may have been difficult to read, and their tone of voice may not have come through, especially if their English was poor.

We NLDers are like you in that foreign country, only we are like that *all the time*, and we are like that in our native country. In some ways, though, it's worse for us, for we are expected to understand the cultural norms and expectations.

When you NTers visit a foreign country, you may misunderstand the gestures, but you know to look for gestures. You will, if you stay a while, start to pick up on all that sort of stuff. We don't, because we can't. We do not pick up on expressive clues or visual mood signals. Our brains just don't work that way.

Another way of thinking about the differences between NLDers and NTers is the things you do automatically are difficult for many of us, like reading facial expressions. Further, while it's difficult to imagine having a learning disability that you don't have, I think it's harder to imagine having an LD in the autism ballpark because it's harder to isolate the challenges.

For example, I read very well. I find it hard to imagine what it's like not to be able to read well. But at least I know what tasks involve reading. It's easy to figure out what jobs a person with dyslexia might have trouble with, and I can even think of some ways around this problem. However it might be difficult to perceive how many ways a person without depth perception is affected in their learning, movement, and daily life. This is difficult for everyone, not only NLDers.

When asked why physics has progressed further than the social sciences, Albert Einstein is reputed to have remarked that physics was much simpler. The predictions of psychologists, teachers, and other professionals are notoriously poor. I don't blame them: We pressure them to make predictions about things that are inherently unpredictable. We'd like to know what the future holds. Like all parents, parents of NLD kids want to know if they will grow up to lead productive, happy lives. Adults with NLD want to know what they can look forward to. Teachers want to know what to prepare their students for. Anyone who tells you they can predict the future of a person is either lying or deluded.

NLDERS: EXCEPTIONS TO THE EXCEPTIONS

As a statistician, I can say what proportion of some particular group, in the past, went on to do what. Statements like "x percent of kids who drop out of high school make minimum wage their whole lives" have some value. But who's to say which percent you or your child is in? Each of us, NLD or not, is an individual. There are exceptions to all the rules, and we NLDers are often exceptions to many rules. **Indeed, we are often the exceptions to the exceptions!** Unfortunately, many NLD adults are underemployed or unemployed despite academic qualifications; I'll talk about some of the reasons for this in Chapter 11. Other NLDers are exceeding everyone's expectations.

There is a Yiddish saying: "Never try to teach a pig to sing; it wastes your time and annoys the pig." The trick is to know when you are trying to teach a pig to sing; it isn't always easy to tell. It is also true that, while any particular person may be good or bad at any particular task, almost anyone can improve at almost anything.

A key question to ask: What is the NLD person's goal? It's one thing to want to play baseball with the Yankees; it's quite another to learn to throw a ball more accurately. The idea that "you can do anything you want to do" is not only incorrect, it's pernicious, because it sets up people for failure rather than success. One way out of this trap is to redefine what you want when engaging in an activity or hobby. Sometimes, the best advice we NLDers can give ourselves or our NLD children is not, "You can do anything you want to do," but "What would success look like to you?"

Of course, there are examples of people who succeeded against tremendous odds. The reason we think these stories are amazing is because they are so rare; there are far more people who tried and failed. This is related to my insistence on calling NLD a "disability"; holding up amazing successes as examples does not do anyone any favors. The list of famous people with various disabilities can inspire but also be intimidating and off-putting.

I have always thought that the correct response to stories such as "Well, Helen Keller was blind and deaf and look how well she did!" is to hold up examples of famous NTers and ask the questioner why *he* isn't more like *that "successful" person*.

If "success" means being like Da Vinci or Einstein, then nearly all of us (including nearly all NTers) are doomed to be failures. But if "success" means making the world better, spreading laughter, and creating joy, then nearly all of us can succeed. It's good to have big dreams; so are little dreams. The little ones are more likely to be fulfilled.

Bill Waterson captures this idea of little dreams in a Calvin and Hobbes cartoon. They are discussing what they would wish for if they could have anything at all. Hobbes wishes for a sandwich. Calvin ridicules this and makes a typically grandiose wish. In the next panel, they are in the kitchen eating and Hobbes says, "I got my wish."

Let me encourage you: NLD is a journey—a difficult, amazing, crazy journey. When you or your child received the diagnosis—or suspected it may describe you—emotions crashed your world like a tsunami. Perhaps you felt numb. Either way, you'll likely go through four stages of accepting NLD.

THE FOUR STAGES OF ACCEPTING NLD
There are, I think, four stages of acceptance of NLD or any disability:

1. There's nothing wrong with me. There must be something wrong with you!
2. There's something wrong with me. Life stinks.
3. There's something wrong with me. You deal with it.
4. There's something wrong with me. I better deal with it.

For short (and for the sake of alliteration), one might call these stages denial, depression, display, and dealing. I don't claim to spend all my time at stage 4; I'd be a lot happier if I could, but I can't, at least not yet. Here, I say more about each of these stages and how I deal with them.

STAGE 1: DENIAL
In stage 1, I was in denial of a difficulty. When things do not go well, I didn't look to what I might be doing badly or how I might do it better; instead, I looked to what others were doing wrong. Often, especially in children, this stage isn't even conscious. Young children often accept themselves as they are

at a primitive level, and any fault must lie elsewhere. In young kids, this is a normal stage. In older kids or adults it is both less normal and less attractive than it is in little kids.

Babies and young kids are natural egotists. They want you to look at them, play with them, and talk to them. They naturally believe that their utterances are interesting, that they are adorable. They are right! Babies *are* adorable. That's what *cute* means. Further, good parents arrange their world so that not too much can go wrong for their babies and little kids. They provide food and a safe environment. Parents don't allow babies to crawl on windowsills or play alone in the tub. Babies don't have to "do as they are told" because adults know that babies don't understand language…yet.

Later in childhood, parents and teachers expect kids to take turns in a conversation, ask about others' feelings, and interact appropriately with kids and adults. At this stage, extreme denial becomes unacceptable.

Development is difficult for all kids; but NT kids have a set of natural guideposts to their development: by their older peers and their families and schools. As tasks gradually get more difficult, NT kids deal with the difficulties. Some kids deal with them better, some worse. For me the difficulties were different in magnitude and type.

What differences in type am I talking about? There are many. My own difficulties can be grouped into difficulties with space and with time. I get lost a lot. (I am glad I live in Manhattan, which is mostly a nice grid with numbered streets—after 78 comes 79!). On my first day of sixth grade I tried to walk to my new school by myself. I had the address. I had been there before. But, an hour after leaving I returned home—I couldn't find the school! At least I found my way home!

STAGE 2: DEPRESSION

In stage 2, I realized something was wrong, but I believed things would never improve, that there was no way to cope with the difficulty, and that no one else shared this difficulty. I was suicidal for much of the time from about age 13 to 17. Once I even sat on a ledge of my room, eight floors above concrete, thinking about jumping. Instead of jumping I wrote a poem:

Have You Ever?

Have you ever been out on a ledge, looking down?
Have you ever felt fear and hate all around?
Have you ever seen warfare inside your own soul?
Have you ever known that you'd never be whole?
And yet for some reason you crawl on back in
Like Hamlet from Shakespeare, but which is the sin?
To jump, fall and die, and thus to be free
Or to be a coward, like Hamlet and me?

I'll share a couple of anti-suicidal strategies. First, let me that if you are suicidal, or you suspect a child you care about is suicidal, seek professional help *immediately*. There are a number of suicide helplines, in the United States, one is 1-800-273-8255. You may wish to share some of the strategies I talk about here with a therapist, but they are not a substitute for therapy. Suicide is *not* a good solution to the problems of NLD or any other LD, and this book is *not* sufficient for dealing with these issues. I'm not a therapist, and even if I was, no book is sufficient for these issues.

Like many NLDers, I am very logical. I can be convinced by logical arguments where emotional ones might fail. In my teen years, I convinced myself not to jump using the irreversibility argument. That is, if I committed suicide, I couldn't ever undo it; but if I did not commit suicide, I could do it some other time.

Many NLDers are good writers, and they may write things down to help them cope. I found writing poetry to be extremely therapeutic. Here is another poem I wrote in my teens.

Gateway to Myself

I dwelt alone, in misery,
A shroud of hate lay over all.
Too alone, and far too fearful,
To let a friend within my wall.
A castle tall and strong I built
And locked myself within its walls.
With my ego bruised and hurting
From a slew too many falls.
I called myself a better person
Than anyone that I could see
But, deep within, I knew me lying
For deep within myself was me.
With the help of years and teachers
(Many of each, I am afraid)
I began to see that I
Could see my castle be unmade.
My first reaction, dim and fearful
Was to build walls higher still.
But I knew myself unhappy
And, somehow, I knew my own will.
Those walls remain, they'll never vanish
Too much pain remains in me
Soon though, they will be made smaller
And let in a friend, or thee.

STAGE 3: DISPLAY

In stage 3, I was aware of my difficulty and began to acknowledge it to myself and others. I realized that I needed to cope with some of the difficulties, but I believed it was the responsibility of other people to cope with them too. I would often talk at great length about my NLD to anyone who would listen to me. One of the problems associated with NLD is that I'm often poor at determining who wants to hear about us NLDers (and who doesn't), with whom it would be inappropriate to discuss my disability, and (in some cases) who would be dangerous to talk to. In addition, at this stage I often thought that once I had told someone about my difficulty, he or she would be eager and able to accommodate me. Often, this was not the case.

The display stage also illustrates another NLD-related problem of mine: determining levels of friendship. NTers move from casual acquaintance to deep friendship gradually, following a series of steps in which more trust is earned and awarded. NTers have many more acquaintances than close friends. Nonverbal cues aid them in moving along this path. How does a person's face look, and how does their voice sound, and what body language are they using, when they talk to you? These are vital cues to levels of friendship, and they are very hard for me and many other NLDers to understand. People do not say, *in words*, "I'd like to be your acquaintance, but I really don't want to be your friend" or "I enjoy hanging out with you once in a while, but not all the time." Rather they *say* these things through tone, body language, and facial expression.

Most NTers want to be polite, so they don't say "no" when confronted directly. They also do not understand that I do not understand body language and so on. In fact, they are likely unaware of how they read and give nonverbal cues. So, when I misunderstand NTers, they may not able to explain what cues they were giving. If you misunderstand a word, you can look the meaning later or ask what it means. This is not an option when you misunderstand (or completely miss) nonverbal communication.

Stage 4: Dealing

When I am in stage 4, I accept my NLD and also know that it is my responsibility to cope with my difficulties and that few people are interested in hearing all about me. Further, when I do tell an appropriate person about NLD-related difficulties, I do not expect him or her to drop everything else in order to cope with me. Stage 4 is the only mature stage, and it is by far the most effective stage for having a successful life. As I said, though, I don't manage to stay at this stage all the time. But, then, NT people, even mature, sensible, well-adjusted NT people, don't act maturely all the time, either.

The extent to which you (or the NLDer in your life) can reach and stay at Stage 4 will, I think, have a huge impact on life and happiness. But I haven't figured out the secrets of doing so.

For Parents: Grief and the Expected Child

Many books on parenting special needs children discuss grief. I do not, except in this brief section. The grief over the child that might have been can last a long time. When a woman becomes pregnant, she and her spouse or partner rarely imagine that the child will have significant problems. They may imagine a "dream child," some ideal combination of the best traits of the parents and their parents.

At first parents of NLD children may deny there's a problem. When the child's difficulties become too obvious to ignore, the parents are confronted with the death, not of the child, but of the dream child. And the real child is a constant reminder that the dream child does not exist. If there are siblings before or after this child is born, it may increase or periodically reinforce the very real loss of the "dream child." Some of this is probably natural, and even helpful.

But if this grief process becomes overwhelming, or lasts too long, then the parents should seek professional help. I am not a therapist, and not qualified to offer this sort of help. I can, however, show ways that your child, NLD and all, is another sort of dream. He or she may never be what you imagined; on the other hand, parenting such a child has its own rewards and joys. Children are amazing creatures. In some ways, children with disabilities are even more amazing than those without them. But parenting such children can be more difficult than parenting NT kids. I have two perspectives on this: Not only am I an NLD adult, and therefore a former NLD child, but one of my own kids has NLD, or something like it, so I am a parent of an NLDer as well.

Although this book is primarily about tweens, teens and adults with NLD, I think that much of it has value for parents of younger kids. First, you may like to see what some people with learning disabilities become. We don't all make tremendous successes of our lives, at least if you define success in terms of making a lot of money or having a high-powered job. Then again, most NT people also don't succeed in this way either. The average person is average; that's what average means. There are lessons parents of young NLD kids can learn from those of us who went before. Second, your young NLD child will, sooner than you think, be a teenager, so you might want to get prepared. You may help your child avoid a difficult school experience socially by teaching social skills. These social skills will help when he or she has a career and functions on their own.

I'll offer this bit of advice here: Your kid is not doing it on purpose. Whatever "it" is…the social miscues, the linear responses when you seek relational communication. You kid's mind works the way it works, and it's not easy to be different. He or she did not ask to be born with NLD and is coping as best as he can.

We all seek to be valued for who we are, as we are. You're coping as best you can as well. Try to take it easy on yourself and on your kids; a short essay to read when you're parenting a special needs kid is "Welcome to Holland," written by Emily Perl Kingsley, a mom of a special needs child. (Read the entire essay at http://www.our-kids.org/Archives/Holland.html.)

Here are a few sentences:

> *"Holland?!?" you say. "What do you mean Holland?? I signed up for Italy! I'm supposed to be in Italy. All my life I've dreamed of going to Italy."*

> *But there's been a change in the flight plan. They've landed in Holland and there you must stay.*

Yes, as Kingslsey says, even if you wind up in Holland, you can still enjoy the trip.

3: What Is NLD? Part 2

THERE ARE MANY DEFINITIONS OF NLD. PARTS OF THIS SECTION are a little technical; you may want to read this section thoroughly or skim it. In Resources, page 159, you'll see a list of the books written by these researchers. Consider reading a book or two. Let's take a look at the definitions.

ROURKE'S DEFINITION

Byron Rourke (1995) was one of the first to study NLD, and he defined it precisely and narrowly. He gave eleven technical criteria for NLD; an advantage is its precision but it may seem formal so I've added explanations and examples:

1. *Bilateral tactile-perceptual deficits, usually more marked on the left side of the body.* NLDers have trouble getting information from sense of touch, especially on the left side. We tend to have unusual sensitivity or lack of it. For instance, while seated at my desk, I may lean forward to look at my computer screen and fail to notice that I am banging my chest on the desk. Another example is my scratching one mosquito-bitten leg with the other without realizing and creating a sore that became infected. Many NLDers also have symptoms of sensory integration dysfunction (Whitney, 2002).

2. *Bilateral psychomotor coordination deficiencies and complex psychomotor skills, especially required within a novel framework, tend to worsen relative to age-based norms.* We have trouble learning all sorts of physical activities, including normal milestones, often walking late. (One child I know walked at age 19 months, the day before his pediatrician had set as a time-limit before calling in specialists). Also, toilet training, running, skipping, whistling, and many other physical skills may be delayed or not develop at all.

3. *Outstanding deficiencies in visual-spatial-organizational abilities.* We NLDers do not conceive of space in the same ways as NT people. For instance, when I put down a cup of juice to do something else, I may have no memory a minute later of where I placed the cup, and spend five minutes looking for it. I also have tremendous difficulty giving directions, and I frequently get lost.

4. *Extreme difficulty in adapting to novel and otherwise complex situations, with an overreliance on prosaic, rote behaviors.* Although this is not a particular problem for me, other NLDers may react stereotypically in many situations. For example, an answer to the question "How are you?" elicits different replies when asked by different people in different situations (e.g., Is it asked by a casual acquaintance, a close friend, or a doctor? Is it asked when you are recovering from an illness?).

5. *Marked deficits in nonverbal problem solving, concept-formation, hypothesis testing, etc.* NLDers tend to have a lot of trouble with problems that require visual solutions. How do we get from here to there? What do the assembly instructions mean? To many NLDers, the visual instructions in an IKEA product might as well be in Swedish.

6. *Concept-formation deficits in hypothesis testing and the inability to benefit from positive and negative informational feedback in novel and otherwise complex situations.* That is, people with NLD may not generalize from specific situations to more general ones, even in cases where most people would do so easily. In addition, rewards and punishments for good and bad behavior may not be applied to related situations. An NLD child told not to do something may think that the proscription applies more narrowly than most children would.

7. *Extremely distorted sense of time.* This has at least two aspects: Knowing how long it will take to do something, and knowing how long ago something happened (or in what order things happened). Many NLDers are frequently late; I am always ridiculously early. Even if I have completed a task many times, I overestimate the required amount of time, often dramatically. For example, I have traveled to the various airports in New York City many times, yet I still allow much too much time, sometimes twice as much time as is needed.

   On sequencing, I cannot remember whether I received my Ph.D. before or after our first son was born. (I earned the degree in 1999, he was born in 1996.) Another example: I know that between ages 12 and 17 I was struck by a car and also had an operation on my eyes. I do not know which happened first.

8. *Well-developed rote verbal capacities.* Many NLDers are good at memorizing information presented verbally, although they may not (or may) understand what is memorized.

9. *Much verbosity of a repetitive, straightforward rote nature.* Many NLDers talk a lot without communicating much

information. They don't engage in "small talk," rather, they repeat topics. They also have trouble taking turns listening and speaking in a conversation. There can also be an Asperger's-like tendency to be didactic and pedantic.

10. *Difficulty with the fluid use of connectors, segues, and dialogue.* NLDers often jump from subject to subject without realizing that others may not follow their thought processes.

11. *Outstanding relative difficulties in mechanical arithmetic as compared with reading and spelling.* NLDers tend to be worse at arithmetic than at verbal skills like reading and spelling. (My own view is that this deficit may be due to the way arithmetic is taught, which often relies highly on visual cues.)

PALOMBO'S DEFINITION

Joseph Palombo (2006) offers more recent clinical definitions. His briefer definition: NLD is "a developmental brain based disorder that impairs a child's capacity to perceive, express and understand nonverbal (nonlinguistic) signs. The disorder is generally expressed as a pattern of impaired functioning in the nonverbal domain, with higher functioning in the verbal domain. The neuropsychological deficits associated with this disorder constrain children's capacity to function in the academic, social, emotional, or vocational domain and lead to a heterogeneous set of neurobehavioral symptoms. The brain dysfunctions affect children's behaviors, their social interactions, their feelings about themselves and others, and their emerging personality patterns–all of which may manifest as symptomatic behaviors."

Palombo stresses the heterogeneity of NLD, and notes that "no single child will display all the features of the disorder."

Except for being specific to children, I like this definition. NLD can and does affect people of every age.

Heterogeneous is a fancy way of stating that "when you've seen one person with NLD, you've seen one person with NLD." Palombo believes that there are three major areas that constrain development in people with NLD, each composed of several domains, and that each domain can lead to different types of social impairments in different people. His scheme may be summarized:

- Neurobehavioral
- Nonlinguistic perception
- Attention and executive functioning
- Other
- Social cognition
- Reciprocal social interaction
- Nonverbal language
- Affects
- Intrapersonal
- Mind-sharing
- Self-coherence
- Narrative coherence

MAMEN'S DEFINITION

Mamen (2007) does not offer a formal definition of NLD but she lists a set of presenting issues, which can be paraphrased as follows:

- Strengths in verbal areas
- Problems with sensory input and higher levels of sensitivity (however, note that some NLDers have lower sensitivity)
- Clumsiness and physical coordination issues

- Problems with hand-eye coordination (visual-motor integration, in her more formal language)
- Fine motor problems
- Executive functioning issues
- Liking for routine and complaints with changes in routine
- Organizational issues
- Social problems, including or arising from problems with nonverbal aspects of speech, problems with personal space.
- Spatial issues
- Problems with concepts related to time, space and distance

WHITNEY'S DEFINITON
Rondalyn Varney Whitney (2002) defined NLD:

My own, very brief definition is that NLD is a learning disability that is primarily nonverbal. This includes difficulties with time, space, visual perception, coordination, sensory integration, and much else.

Whitney also notes that, in her view, a lack of social skills is a part of NLD by definition: "If a child has all the markers of NLD, but has good social skills, she might have another learning disability, but not NLD."

KUTSCHER'S DEFINITION
Martin L. Kutscher (2005) describes NLD as a cluster of symptoms having to do with integrating information, especially nonverbal information, in three main areas:

- **Motor skills** including both

  ° **Gross motor skills.** Many NLDers reach developmental

milestones late and have problems with gross motor
skills throughout their lives. Difficulty walking, running, climbing, or riding a bike may lead to hesitancy
in exploring things physically.

- **Fine motor skills.** Difficulty with all small motions
shows up in handwriting and holding and grasping
small objects. For example, my own handwriting is so
poor that I flunked written spelling tests, but proved
difficult to stump in an oral spelling bee.

- **Visual/spatial orientation skills** and an inability to form
mental pictures. NLDers often label everything verbally
and attempt to use verbal skills to handle visual and spatial information. They also have difficulty knowing where
they are in space and frequently get lost or have trouble
navigating, even in familiar places. For example in 1977
there was a blackout in New York City. I had lived in the
same room for ten years. Yet, I could not find my way
out of my room in the dark. Or, as another example, in
childhood, being blindfolded terrified me. I think this is
because I had little visual memory to go on.

    This is one thing that distinguishes many NLDers
from many people with Asperger's or high-functioning
autism. Temple Grandin has often written that she thinks
in pictures—she even titled one of her books *Thinking in
Pictures*—and this appears to be typical of people with
autism, and (perhaps to a lesser degree) of people with
Asperger's. We NLDers, on the other hand, think in words.

- **Social/communication skills** which lead to great problems making friends, despite the desire to do so. Kutscher
notes that while NLDers desire friendship, many people
with Asperger's do not *appear* to want friends. My own

view is that people vary on a continuum of how much they want to be alone and how many friends they want. At one end, you have hermits who live almost completely alone. At the other, you have people who are around others all the time. Most people, whether AS, NLD, or NT, are somewhere between these extremes. I have noticed, however, that many NLD people need time alone each day in ways that most NT people do not. Particular problems common in NLD, according to Kutscher, include:

° Being overly focused on details
° Trouble integrating non-verbal and verbal information
° Being very literal
° Seeing things in black and white
° Gullibility
° Trouble reading social cues, which can lead to appearing rude, self-centered, or weird.

NLD DESCRIBES, IT DOES NOT DEFINE

Disabilities often come in cluster diagnoses. The current practice of professionals is to identify "cluster" behaviors or identification processes since many overlap in diagnosis. There are a number of diagnoses that have symptoms or areas of difficulty in common with NLD.

Often NLD is lumped "on the spectrum" of behaviors with autism. I agree that autism is a socially affected disability but NLD is truly a world of its own. Some people may argue whether some of these disabilities are separate from NLD at all. I don't intend to join that argument. I think we know so little about all these diagnoses that such arguments are pointless.

Furthermore, many people have symptoms of several syndromes or disorders, so a single diagnosis may be inappropriate.

Still, we humans do like to label things, and it is not entirely a bad idea to do so. Getting the "right" diagnosis can help you get the best resources for your needs. Just remember that you are you. If something works for you, it works for you, whether it is "supposed" to work for NLD or not, and regardless of where you read about it. Similarly, if something does *not* work for you, it doesn't, regardless of how well it works for someone else, or how many people it has worked for.

Bearing in mind the problems of diagnosing people, it may nonetheless be useful to distinguish NLD from other syndromes and conditions. Kutscher gives some valuable and relatively short sets of symptoms of various syndromes. I elaborate on these here, emphasizing similarities to and differences from NLD.

NLD vs. Autism

Autistic spectrum disorders. The current version of the *Diagnostic and Statistical Manual of Mental Disorders* (DSM-V) classifies NLD as one of the autistic spectrum disorders. Certainly, there are some commonalities among autism, Asperger's syndrome, and NLD. All involve one form or another of communication problems. They differ in which particular parts of communication are problematic, the extent of the problems, and the other problems that are present. We may make the following distinctions, based on the work of Kutscher and Palombo:

Autistic disorder is marked by severe problems with verbal and nonverbal communication and highly unusual behaviors.

Asperger's syndrome (AS) involves relatively good verbal language, with problems in nonverbal communication and a restricted range of interests and problems with relatedness (Kutscher, 2005) and includes autistic features that are not present in NLD (Palombo, 2006). In addition, one distinguishing characteristic of NLD is tactile imperceptions, such as difficulty recognizing objects they are holding with their eyes closed or identifying letters drawn on their backs or fingers; Whitney (2002) says these are rarely found in AS but are always found in NLD.

AUTISM: IT'S NOT A SPECTRUM; IT'S A BALLPARK

When I was getting my Master's in education, "autism" meant a specific type of syndrome–think *Rain Man*. Nowadays, people with a wide variety of problems, and a wide variety of levels of problem, are called some variety of "autism." There's "high functioning autism" and (as noted above) the DSM-V moved Asperger's Syndrome and NLD to the spectrum. Autism spectrum is a pervasive term; I've even used it myself.

The most famous use of the word "spectrum" is probably the color spectrum: red, orange, yellow, green, blue, indigo and violet. Wavelength determines a color's place on the spectrum. Of course, the spectrum does not fully describe a color. To fully describe a color you need three attributes–you can use hue, saturation and value (HSV), or red, green, blue (RGB), or other methods. But it's not just one dimension.

WHY "AUTISM SPECTRUM" IS MISLEADING

"Spectrum" implies a high degree of order, but the autism spectrum is not like this! As noted, autism involves many aspects of behavior and thought and interaction; if you add the other "autism spectrum disorders" the range is even broader.

How can we put all ASD people on a spectrum? If someone has severe deficits socially, but communicates halfway OK in some situations, and has no specific movements, is he farther along the spectrum than someone who has moderate social deficits but has a lot of repetition of movement? What if one of the people hyper-focuses and the other doesn't? Who knows! That's because it's not a spectrum.

Psychologists and others probably like "spectrum." It sounds like science, and it implies that they know what they are talking about. Maybe some of these psychologists have what has been called "physics envy" I think that's all wrongheaded. Psychology isn't physics, and physics isn't psychology. Psychologists shouldn't try to be like physicists, they should try to be better psychologists.

IT'S MORE LIKE AN AUTISM BALLPARK

For all the research (and it's been valuable), we are still in the infancy of learning about autism and related syndromes. I doubt that "spectrum" will ever be appropriate—psychology is too complex—but it certainly isn't appropriate now. So, what term should we use?

Ballpark!

Look at a baseball field. There's a center that spreads out in all directions. Then we could say that a person with all the symptoms of classic autism is, say, standing on second base, in the middle of the field. Other people might be out in left field, or on the pitcher's mound, or in left field. Take me: I have some symptoms of autism, some symptoms of Asperger's some symptoms of NLD; I have a 100 percent diagnosis of being me. Maybe I don't belong on the autism spectrum, but I am in the ballpark!

By the way, the classic definition of NLD includes a lack of sense of humor. If you think that I think that's sort of silly—well, you're in the ballpark!

I AM NOT TEMPLE GRANDIN, AND I AM NOT AUTISTIC

Temple Grandin is famous; perhaps the most famous autistic person in the world. She's written books, has a career, and a Ph.D.–it's amazing. But she's autistic. I'm not. What are the differences between her (and some other people with autism) and me (and some other people with NLD)?

When people hear about NLD, they think it sounds a lot like Asperger's syndrome (and there are similarities). And Asperger's is, often, described as a form of autism (and there are similarities). Remember the saying "When you've seen one person with NLD, you've seen one person with NLD"? The same is true about autism; not all people with autism are like Temple Grandin. Here I use myself as an example of a person with NLD; other people with nonverbal learning disabilities are different from me.

Some dissimilarities between me and many autistic people:

Many autistic people (not all) like animals. Most notably, Temple Grandin really likes animals. I don't like animals. I don't get them. When I'm dealing with people, I deal better with purely verbal information–words, whether written or spoken. And, except possibly for dolphins and some highly trained apes, animals don't talk. Certainly none of them speak English. People who get along with animals rely on nonverbal cues, just the sort of thing I'm bad at. Many people (NT or autistic or whatever) get a lot of pleasure out of stroking a dog or cat. I don't. I don't hate doing it, but it doesn't give me joy.

Many autistic people (not all) think in pictures. Temple Grandin wrote a book called *Thinking in Pictures*. I do not think in pictures. Not at all. Not nearly as much as a typical NT person. I think in words and sometimes in symbols. Unlike many people who are not visual, I am good at math (I'm a statistician), and relate better to algebra than to geometry. In childhood, when I learned arithmetic I didn't memorize stuff, I made up tricks; the visual explanation of multiplication did nothing for me–I thought of it as repeated addition. Mamen (2007) points out the importance of visualization not just in terms of math but also in developing social skills. She also notes that visualization can be about the past (e.g., when we need to recall the image of a word, a face, or any other visual information), the present (e.g., when we need to recognize people's faces and many objects), and the future.

These problems with visualization are one of the cores of many of the problems NLDers can have. Whitney (2002) notes that they can relate to poor visual recall, poor spatial abilities, difficulties with writing the alphabet, difficulties with visual art (both creating it and appreciating it), problems with physical coordination, safety issues, and a general sense of clumsiness.

Many autistic people are good at certain types of routine physical tasks–things like spinning a top, or sometimes spinning themselves. I am not good at any of this. Of course, in some ways, that makes me atypical for NLD as well as for autism. I'm typical of me. The only diagnosis that fits me perfectly is "Peter."

PDD-NOS is "pervasive development disorder, not otherwise specified" and is a catch-all term for nonverbal problems that do not meet criteria for other disorders. In Kutscher's scheme, based on the DSM-IV, these PDD-NOS include the following:

- **High functioning autism** which some use as a synonym for Asperger's, and others use to refer to people who have milder autism with no retardation.
- **NLD,** the subject of this book, which he describes as "trouble integrating information in three areas: nonverbal difficulties causing the [person] to miss the major gestalt in language, spatial perception problems; and motor coordination problems." It often involves sensory integration dysfunction.
- **Semantic pragmatic language disorder** which involves delays in both semantic and pragmatic language, but

few problems in socialization. NLD, in contrast, does *not* involve problems with semantic language, and usually involves problems with socialization.

NLD vs. Other Diagnoses

One reason it is important to distinguish NLD from other conditions is treatment may vary. Importantly, some methods that work well with one condition may work badly with NLD and vice versa. In order to recognize misdiagnosis we have to learn a bit about the other diagnoses. In addition, NLD can co-exist with other conditions.

ADHD, which stands for attention deficit hyperactivity disorder, is (according to the DSM-IV) of three types:

1. Primarily inattentive
2. Primarily hyperactive-impulsive
3. Combined

Non-verbal learning disabilities share some characteristics with ADHD, including problems with executive functioning, which includes the ability to inhibit actions, working memory (as opposed to long-term memory), foresight, hindsight, organization and planning, self-talk, sense of time, coping with transitions from one activity to another, and separating fact from emotion. Many of these problems are common in NLD as well; but many NLDers have an unusual type of problem with attention: They are often distracted by internal thoughts.

Whereas someone with ADHD may stop doing one thing in order to do another, and then change again a moment later, stop doing something and seem to be doing noth- people are distracted by seeing a butterfly outside NLDers are distracted by *thinking* about butterflies.

For example, I knew a boy with NLD who would brush his teeth and then sit in a chair with the toothbrush still in his mouth. He would start thinking about something and simply forget he was brushing his teeth, but that "something" that he was thinking about would be entirely internal.

Also, many NLDers excel at talking themselves through problems, and may, in fact, rely on this tactic to solve many problems, even those where NT people would not need to self-talk.

Symptoms of ADHD that Kutscher says are more common in older children and adults include the following (most are not common among most NLDers):

1. *Getting angry frequently and quickly.* This is not common in NLD.

2. *Pushing away those whose help they need most.* I have not noticed this being common in NLD, but many NLDers are comfortable alone, need alone time each day, and are easily overwhelmed by the stimuli involved in interacting with others. NLDers may also misinterpret offers of help.

3. *Hyper-responsiveness, or having excessive emotions.* I think that a lot of NLDers appear this way. But some (perhaps more) can appear the opposite way: unemotional and unresponsive. This arises, I think, because emotions are transmitted primarily nonverbally. We don't say "I am angry" or "I am sad" or, for that matter "I am happy" nearly as often as we communicate those emotions through body language, tone, facial expression, and acting out. Yet NLDers have problems both with expressive and receptive nonverbal language. I know many NLDers who say that other people tell them they appear angry or sad when they are actually not feeling that way. While with most people, the face is a pathway to someone's true

feelings, with us, it is not. We must be taught to be aware of how we utilize facial expressiveness.

4. *Inflexibility and explosive reactions.* This is sometimes a problem with NLD people, particularly when plans are changed.

5. *Feeling calm when in motion.* I believe that this may be a key distinguishing factor. Most NLDers seem to be more comfortable when still, and find rapid or quickly changing motions disturbing (e.g., many NLDers cannot abide amusement park rides, some get various types of motion sickness). These problems are also symptomatic of people with sensory integration problems, who may either seek a lot of motion, or be unusually averse to it.

6. *Thrill-seeking.* Again, I do not believe this is common in NLD. In fact, in a completely unscientific poll I did, most NLDers said they were *less* tolerant of thrills than most NTers. This may relate to symptoms of sensory integration disorder, or to problems orienting ourselves in space and time. For many NLD people, the "ordinary" world is overwhelming; attempts to increase that are often not welcome.

7. *Trouble paying attention to others.* This can certainly happen in NLD, as well.

8. *Trouble with mutual exchanges of favors with friends.* This can be problematic for NLDers, but primarily, I think, because of the difficulties with reading all the cues that go into reading another person.

9. *Sense of failure to achieve goals.* This is, I think, common with NLD.

10. *Lying, cursing, and blaming others.* I do not think this is common in NLD.

According to Whitney (2002) the stimulants that are often used to treat ADHD are counterproductive in NLD. Although many NLD people fidget, they do so for different reasons than ADHD people.

Dyslexia involves difficulty with reading. NLDers are not typically dyslexic. In fact, many NLDers read quite early. NLDers do, however, often have problems with certain parts of reading, especially drawing inferences and keeping track of complex plots. Many NLDers prefer nonfiction to fiction; or, if they like fiction, prefer relatively simple narrative styles. I have also noticed that many NLD people have trouble reading aloud. Reading aloud involves a complex combination of tasks that we tend to be bad at: tone of voice and related issues, as well as the sheer coordination involved in reading aloud.

Dyscalculia or difficulty with math, is present in some NLDers, but absent in others, who may be gifted in math, as I am. Particular areas of math tend to be hard for NLDers, especially geometry and the physical applications of calculus.

According to Rourke's criteria, difficulty with math is a distinguishing feature of NLD, but I have known many NLDers for whom this is not the case. In addition, most people who are good at math are spatial and visual, but there is a subset of mathematically minded people for whom this is not the case. This may lead to misdiagnosis of dyscalculia. This is one of the areas where I think the syndrome has evolved away from Rourke's original definition to a more inclusive one.

Language LD. Mamen (2007) divides LDs into NLD and LLD, where the latter stands for "language learning disabilities." This is a nice division; it is intuitively clear (and makes it clearer what "NLD" means). But it overlooks the fact that the nonverbal aspects of language are a fundamental part of NLD.

LD involving writing can involve problems with spelling,

grammar, punctuation, and handwriting. In my experience, nearly all NLDers have problems with handwriting, and these may be so severe as to appear to be problems with the other areas; however, these other areas are not usually problematic in themselves. Many NLDers do have problems organizing longer written work.

LD, not specified is a sort of catch-all for people who don't fit elsewhere.

Developmental coordination disorder (DCD) refers to unskillful or clumsy performance of motor skills. Most NLDers do have problems with motor skills. Many NLDers are also hypotonic, that is, they have low muscle tone. However, NLDers have a number of other difficulties, which DCD people do not.

Mental retardation refers to significant problems in *overall* intelligence. This is quite distinct from learning disabilities, which refer to problems in *particular* areas.

Oppositional defiance disorder (ODD), in children, is a disorder of an ongoing pattern of uncooperative, defiant, and hostile behavior toward authority figures. Some ODD symptoms may include:

- Frequent temper tantrums
- Excessive arguing with adults
- Often questioning rules
- Active defiance and refusal to comply with adult requests and rules
- Deliberate attempts to annoy or upset people
- Blaming others for his or her mistakes or misbehavior
- Spiteful attitude and revenge seeking

I was such a child, although I never got a formal diagnosis of ODD. I had *all* of these traits to one degree or another.

Why would a child act this way? Why did I?

There can be many reasons, including neurological problems. But in my case, at least, a lot of my defiance and opposition was an attempt to define myself in a hostile world and to organize the overwhelming flood of information when unable to process the way neuro-typical children do. I *still* use it to organize knowledge.

Let's look at two parts of the description in the previous paragraph.

Define myself in a hostile world.

There is a scene in the movie *The Paper* in which one character (Henry) asks "When did you start getting so paranoid?" and the other (Michael McDougal) replies, "When everyone started plotting against me." This is how the world can seem to LD people, especially in childhood. Kids, and especially kids in the autism ballpark, have difficulty distinguishing active hostility from the failed attempts of some well-meaning people to "get us." For me, the world was largely made up of people who were against me. If you experience everyone else as hostile and oppositional, then reacting with hostility and opposition isn't a disorder, it's adaptive.

Organize the overwhelming flood of information that I was unable to process.

Many LD children and adults have difficulty processing information, or particular types of information. I never learned to take notes, but I was quick at figuring out opposing points of view. (In high school, I once had a debate with myself!) This is a way of organizing information. In order to figure out why what the teacher is saying is *wrong*, you have to understand what the teacher is saying. Once you've understood it, it's a lot easier to remember.

There are other reasons for apparent defiance: Whitney (2002) points out that many NLD kids may appear defiant when they simply failed to understand a request, often because they took your words literally or did not understand the nonverbal cues. One example is the question that isn't a question. If you say "Would you like to clean up your room?" and your NLD child says "No," he is not necessarily being defiant–he answered your question!

There are other signs to distinguish NLD from ODD: Look at your child when he or she is being oppositional or defiant. Is he enjoying himself? Is he happy? Is she having a good time? If the honest answers are yes, then something else is going on. But usually the answer is a clear "no." If your child isn't enjoying a behavior, why does she keep engaging in it? It must be something else; it may be that the alternative feels worse.

What Does the D in NLD Mean?

In the Preface, I mentioned that I use the D in NLD to mean disabled, or disability. Not only do I think that this accurately reflects the nature of NLD and its effects on those of us who have it, but I think calling it "learning differences" demeans us, and may be harmful. As a parent, I can understand that a dad or mom does not want to tell a child that he or she is disabled. But the discovery of a diagnosis can be a great relief. People with NLD are often described as lazy, crazy, or stupid; sometimes, they feel this way about themselves.

Even young children can sense that they are different from their peers, that other kids their age can do things that they cannot, and that they seem to miss things that other people get. If the child's parents attempt to minimize these difficulties by not being frank with their children, the children may internalize a worse self-image than they would have had if they were labeled. Children who are told that they are "different" may assume their difficulties *are* signs that they are lazy, crazy, or stupid. NLDers can sometimes learn how to overcome parts of their disabilities, just as a legless child may be taught to walk with the use of prosthetics; however, to say that if they try hard enough they will have "natural legs" would be cruel. Such is the case with calling what is truly a disability a learning difference.

Although NLDers have a stereotype that they lack a sense of humor, this is not really true. It may apply more to humor that is visual and less to humor that is verbal; also, in an informal poll, I found that almost no NLDers find "practical jokes" funny. Whitney (2002) reports on her son and other NLD kids she sees having a great sense of humor; indeed, she and her son laugh about "NLD moments"—this is only possible because she told him his diagnosis. Of course, you should carefully *explain* the diagnosis; that it doesn't make your child a bad person or incapable of learning, but that some things may be difficult or even impossible, and that she may need to learn in a different way from most kids.

Another reason for using "disability" rather than "different" is that children who are simply "different" do not get protected by legally required accommodations for learning in school, including special services. Without testing, evaluation, and identification of a learning disability, many students miss out on an appropriate education. Everyone is different; some of us are disabled.

Person with NLD? NLDer? What?

Some people in the learning disability community (often the ones who insist on calling it a learning difference) dislike the term "learning-disabled person" and prefer "person with a learning disability." They often also object to describing a person as "learning disabled." I am not such a person. These people are acting in what they perceive as the best interests of us, the learning disabled.

Why do they object to these terms?

I certainly don't want to speak for all of them, but the explanations I hear most often are something like "the person is not a learning disability" or "learning disability does not define the person." Indeed not. I certainly agree that I am not a learning disability! I am a person. I also agree that being learning disabled does not define me. It *describes* me, but only partially. No one word defines anyone!

But there are other adjectives–including adjectives for disabilities and for stigmatized groups–that do not get treated this way.

I am nearsighted. No one calls me a "person with myopia"!

There are various terms for members of ethnic groups. For example, some people prefer "Black," some prefer "African American" and some prefer another term But no one says "person with blackness"!

Nor does anyone get called "person with gayness" or "person with homosexuality."

So, call me learning disabled. Or call me a learning-disabled person. Or call me an LDer. If you insist, you can call me a person with learning disability.

Or, just call me Peter.

4: What Are Nonverbal Aspects of Communication?

IN THE MEDIA, YOU'VE SEEN VARIOUS NUMBERS QUOTED IN VARious places about how much information is communicated verbally and nonverbally. I don't think the exact numbers are important. I'm not even sure they are meaningful. I don't know if you can divide meaning up that way. But nonverbal communication is clearly important. To see how important it is, try watching a favorite TV show with the sound turned off. You still get quite a lot, don't you? Now try watching the show with your eyes closed. Even if it's a show where people don't move around much, you miss a lot, right? That's how we NLD people are. **We watch life with our eyes closed.** We miss a lot.

Nonverbal communication can be divided into several sorts of skills; different authors divide it slightly differently, Duke and his colleagues (1996) divide it like this:

- Paralanguage
- Facial expression
- Space and touch
- Gestures and postures
- Rhythm and speed of speech
- Objectics

PARALANGUAGE

Paralanguage includes all the aspects of sound that accompany speech: tone, volume, rate of speech, and nonverbal sound patterns (all the ums, uhs, and so on while speaking). Paralanguage is especially important when you cannot see the person you are talking to, for instance, on the telephone.

Children respond to tone of voice before they learn any vocabulary. *Tone* of voice is critical in communicating such things as sarcasm, and, on a more basic level, to telling the difference between a simple statement: "John is late," an angry exclamation: "John is late!" or a question, "John is late?" Many NLD people have problems both with understanding tone and with producing the appropriate tone. The former leads confuses NLDers; the latter may lead to conflict between what NLDers are saying and how they say it. For example, saying "Have a good day!" in an angry tone is likely to confuse the person you are talking to. Tone of voice communicates emotions such as anger, sadness, happiness, or excitement.

Volume communicates emotions, you wouldn't shout "Will you marry me?" to your intended while seated across the table from him or her, nor would you whisper "fire!" in a crowded theater.

Nonverbal sound refers to all the *noises* we make while speaking that aren't words. Sounds like "Uh-huh" for yes and "Uh-uh" for no. Notice how similar these are yet NT people hear the difference without a problem. "Mmm-mmm-mmm" can be a warning (when the second part is louder than the first, and the third is in a rising-falling pitch) or a sound of delight. NLD people can have trouble hearing these differences.

Rate of speech varies from person to person and from culture to culture. For example, people from the southern United States often speak more slowly than people from New York City. NT people use rate of speech to communicate meaning; and they also read meaning into rate of speech. Slow speech can be soothing (as when a parent tries to calm an upset child) but it can also make the speaker appear ignorant or nervous (as when someone speaks slowly when called on in class). Contrariwise, rapid speech can excite people and can make the speaker appear knowledgable, but it can also confuse people. Slower speech is also used when explaining something. Faster speech can express confidence, or it can express being rushed or nervous. Combined with loudness, it can indicate an emergency. NT people vary their rates of speech easily and unconsciously, but NLD people may have a lot of trouble with this.

Emphasis and variation can radically change the meaning of a sentence. Duke, Nowicki and Martin (1996) give the following illustration (which I changed a little): Take the sentence "I didn't say John took my money." This sentence can mean at least seven different things.

- That you didn't say John took your money.
- That someone else said that John took your money.
- That you were misquoted
- That, although you didn't *say* John took it, you think he did.
- That you said someone other than John took your money.
- That you loaned or gave John money
- That John took someone else's money.
- That John took something else of yours.

How can it mean all these different things? Try saying the sentence first with no emphasis, and then emphasizing each different word.

FACIAL EXPRESSION

Many people with nonverbal learning disorders have difficulty recognizing facial expressions. Some of us don't deduce information or recognize them at all. Others may recognize the basic emotions (e.g., happiness, anger, fear, sadness) especially in photographs, but have difficulty doing this in "real time" and with more subtle emotions. Faces express intensity of emotion too.

NLDers have difficulty understanding these differences. A young NLDer played with a computer game from Sesame Street. He mastered most of the activities easily, but one asked him to paste eyes, a nose, and mouth on Elmo to make a "happy," "sad," or "angry" face, and he had enormous problems with this. Among the basic emotions, Duke et al (1996) found that happy faces are easier to recognize than fearful, sad or angry ones. This may be because happiness is the only one of these that results in an upturned mouth.

The difficulty with reading facial expression creates confusion. Imagine the confusion caused by someone speaking excitedly but with a bored or expressionless face. Or the confusion felt by someone unable to interpret facial expressions of others. In addition, research shows that people who tend to have happy faces are more socially successful (Duke et al, 1996); they also tend to make more eye contact (a difficulty many NLD people have). Duke et al (1996) offer exercises to improve both receptive and expression facial expression. See Resources, page 154.

SPACE, DISTANCE, AND TOUCH

The use of space and distance in communication is called "proxemics." The amount of space we expect varies by situation. It's one thing to be shoved next to a person on a crowded bus or subway;

it's quite different to have this happen on an empty bus or train. Neuro-typical people learn personal space as part of growing up. Many NLD people do not.

Most cultures seem to have four zones of personal space, which Duke et al (1996) call intimate, personal, social, and public. In the United States, public space is about 3 to 5 feet, social is about 2 feet, personal is about 1 foot and anything closer is intimate (LaVoie, 1996). Violations of these rules can cause intense anxiety; and that anxiety may be unfocused. Unless the space violation is extreme, the bothered person may not even know what is causing his anxiety. In extreme cases, personal space violations may be viewed as harassment.

Fortunately, these rules are easy to verbalize: "Don't stand closer than arm's length to someone, unless you are forced to or unless you are very close friends," for example. Unfortunately, there are many rules. Some rules are complex and difficult to verbalize clearly. For example, a hug is an intimate gesture as is a kiss. But different hugs are differently intimate and a kiss on the cheek is not a kiss on the lips. (And, again, different cultures do all these things differently—just compare how most Italians greet each other to how most Americans do.) Also, back to front or side to side space is less intimate than front to front space, which is one reason people in a crowded elevator will all stand facing forward (unless they are in conversation).

Touch also varies across situations and cultures. But the same touch feels quite different if it is accidental or deliberate; if it is from a stranger, an associate, a friend, a teammate, a doctor, or a lover. To take an extreme example, touching a woman's breast could be offensive (from a stranger or associate) or delightful (from a lover) or medical (from a doctor) or invitational (from someone who is not *yet* a lover) or just embarrassing (if it is not from a doctor or lover but is purely accidental).

The use of space, distance, and touch is also key to *forming* friendships and changing their level of intimacy–an area that many NLDers have trouble with.

If a child does these things wrong, he will probably be ostracized by his peers (LaVoie, 1996) but if a teacher asks the other kids what he is doing wrong, they may not even *know*. Instead they will say something like "he's a dork," which is not very helpful. So, if you are a teacher or parent, observe how an ostracized kid uses space–you may notice things that none of the kids do.

GESTURES AND POSTURES

Gestures and postures are similar in that they communicate at a distance. A difference is that postures are inevitable. We always adapt one posture or another, while gestures are, if not exactly deliberate, at least somewhat voluntary. Another difference is that gestures involve only part of the body (most often the hands) while postures involve the entire body.

NTers use a huge array of gestures and postures, and they read others' use of these without even thinking about it. One way to concentrate your attention on gestures is, again, to watch a movie or TV show with the sound off. But here this exercise is incomplete, because, often, gestures are used to accentuate and explicate the meaning of words.

For example, the word "Stop" has several meanings. As a command, it can mean "stop moving forward" as when warning someone to keep their distance, or it can mean "stop acting that way" as when telling a children that they are out of control. The first meaning might be accompanied by holding your arm straight out with your wrist bent and your fingers up, while the latter might be accompanied by shaking your finger at someone. Use of the right gesture intensifies and clarifies what the word means; use of the wrong gesture leads to confusion.

RHYTHM AND SPEED OF SPEECH

People's speech varies in rhythm and speed in various ways; people from different places tend to speak more or less quickly, but each person will speak more or less quickly in different situations. Most children naturally pick up the patterns of those around them (this is one way that geographical differences are developed and maintained) but NLD children may not.

Many adults are uncomfortable listening to people who speak at a much different pace than they are used to; or with unfamiliar rhythmical patterns. It can be more difficult to understand what they are saying, and we may form impressions of them based on their speech. A child who speaks much faster or slower than her peers, or with a different rhythm, may have social issues. In addition, a child who cannot vary her rate of speech, or who varies it in unorthodox ways, may be viewed as odd.

Many NLDers I know are told that they "sound angry" when they are not. Clearly, sounding angry all the time is not a way to win friends and influence people; it turns people off. Often, these acquaintances will be turned off and not know why, because our reactions to others' rhythm and tone (unless they are extreme) is unconscious. In addition, rhythm and speed of speech may convey emotions or interpersonal messages such as fondness or flirtation. "You are so beautiful" feels different if it is said with pauses between each word or rushed through in a second. I have known several NLD women who say that they are unaware when people are flirting with them, until others tell them.

OBJECTICS

The communication expressed by what we wear, what we own, what cars we drive and so on is called *objectics*, a term coined by Steve Nowicki. Many people with NLD are utterly unaware that they communicate via their clothes, hairstyles, and so on.

However, NLDers can learn about objectics as long as they learn verbally. It often helps if you admit that the rules of objectics are arbitrary and even silly.

TURN TAKING

When we converse, we take turns and the cues to turn taking are nonverbal. Rarely does someone say "you talk now." Equivalents to "you talk now" *do* happen when the nonverbal aspect is blocked–on the phone ("go ahead") or with the classic "over" indicating that the other person should speak. But in regular conversation people look for things like a person taking a breath to indicate they are ready to speak, or a certain tone that indicates finality, or a yawn to indicate that we are going on too long. Unless, of course, we are NLD–in which case we miss those nonverbal cues (Mamen, 2007).

5: Diagnosis and the Mountain of NLD

In medicine, doctors use diagnoses to help them determine appropriate treatment. Treatments are established for many diseases and conditions; what works for one condition may be contraindicated for others. Identifying the correct medical label can be a matter of life and death. If an unconscious person comes into an emergency room, the doctors need to know if he's unconsciousness due to a seizure, a stroke, a drug overdose, a heart attack, or some other problem.

Educators often do not know the appropriate treatment for a particular condition; the definitions are constantly changing; and, what works with one person fails horribly with another. Further, the education plans often are intentionally vague, because they depend on the characteristics of the individual. Diagnosis is, therefore, much less useful in education than in medicine.

Diagnoses and labels have some value for us NLDers. You are reading this book because you are interested in nonverbal learning disabilities. That's a diagnosis and part of this book's title. When you are looking for resources, a label is a great place to start. (Turn to page 159 for a list of resources.) A diagnosis of NLD is not the same as Asperger's or high functioning autism; it's its own thing. But there are significant overlaps with those conditions and others (see Chapter 3).

But, taken too seriously, a label can be a box, and boxes are for groceries, not people. If you, or your child, doesn't fit with some aspect of NLD, then that does not indicate some flaw in you or your child. Rather, it indicates that researchers don't know all that much about these things yet. I have also seen people ask questions such as "Can a child have NLD and ADHD?" My answer is another question: "*Does* your child have NLD and ADHD?" If a child has both, then, clearly, it is possible to have both; if a book says otherwise, the book is wrong.

Take from this book (or any resource) what is helpful to you and the problems you face. Let's concentrate on a strategy for success later in this chapter. I refer to "the mountain." We NLDers need to recognize what can we do well, what we cannot do well, and what we cannot do at all. Then we can use our strengths to get around our difficulties... much of the time.

LUMPING VS. SEPARATING

I am unqualified to say how a formal diagnosis of NLD should be given; indeed, in the DSM-V, NLD is classified as an autism spectrum disorder, and not as its own disorder at all. Here, however, I discuss how parents and teachers can tell informally if a child has NLD. Ultimately, the child is more important than the diagnosis. Professionals who would like details on diagnosing NLD based on test scores may consult Mamen (2007), listed in Resources, page 159.

One issue in diagnosis is "lumping" versus "separating." Should we lump together a huge group of people with issues that don't overlap well? Or should we make smaller groups and have few people in each group? The DSM-V is clearly toward the "lumping" end. Mamen (2007) is near the other end. She distinguishes four subtypes of NLD (see below). I tend to favor the latter because it brings us closer to the individual child; but, in my experience, some people have issues from two or more of the subtypes Mamen defines, so the "lumping" school is not without merit.

Parents may be particularly interested in Mamen's views of "risk factors in preschool children":

- Active avoidance of fine motor activities
- Problems with intelligibility or fluency of speech
- Difficulties with subtle aspects of language (e.g., humor, analogy, symbolic language)
- Poor social use of language
- Hypersensitivity to stimuli
- Problems with gross motor activities
- Eye-hand coordination issues

I list five broad areas that can be problematic for NLD people:

1. Zero order skills
2. Social problems
3. Sensory overload
4. Organization and visual spatial problems
5. Academics

I will deal with the first four here and with academics in Chapter 8.

THE MOUNTAIN — INTRODUCTION

A disability is like a mountain between where you are and where you want to go. There are, I think, four types of responses to this mountain:

1. You can pretend you don't want to get to the other side of the mountain.

2. You can go over the mountain. I think of this as taking extra time to get to the other side.
3. You can go through the mountain. This is making more effort to get to the other side.
4. You can go around the mountain. This is figuring out some path that neuro-typical people often miss.

One of the biggest problems for NLDers is that other people don't see the mountain of NLD. With physical disabilities, such as paraplegia, the disability is *visible*. Unless you are an expert, you may misunderstand how the mountain affects the person (and different people with similar disabilities will be affected in different ways) but you at least know it is there. No learning disability is visible, but NLD (and all the disabilities in the autism ballpark) are what I call *doubly invisible*.

Let's consider broad areas that are problematic for NLDers and use the mountain strategy with each one.

ZERO ORDER SKILLS

Zero order skills are, in Lavoie's phrase, "skills that are only significant when they fail to exist." (Lavoie, 1996). These may be neurological (e.g., clumsiness, poor balance) or social. Social examples include poor hygiene, failure to make or maintain appropriate eye contact, improper conversation—such as saying "nice to meet you" to someone you already know—or difficulty with repeated activities such as tooth brushing or making a bed. Lavoie notes that NT people do these activities in the same way every time, which quickly leads to mastery. He calls these "kinetic melodies." NLDers are notoriously poor at developing these kinetic melodies. LaVoie (1996) notes that one prominent zero order skill is proxemics–the use of space and distance in communication.

Zero order skills also include the inability to focus the eyes without moving the head (LaVoie, 1996), leading to difficulties with reading, especially sentences or paragraphs (but not single words). Other zero order skill deficits are hyper-reactive startles (or over reaction to sudden noises, touches, and so on) or failure to react to such stimuli; attention problems; hyper- and hypo-activity; difficulty with common motor skills; problems with copying from a board; echolalia; and problems with orientation in space. Another set of zero order skills is anything learned automatically such as "tracking people's eye movements."

Again, what these zero order skills have in common is that they are noticed only when they are absent (or, occasionally, when they are present in very high degree). Lacking these skills is a big problem for NLDers.

THE MOUNTAIN AND ZERO ORDER SKILLS

Giving Up
Giving up is not really an option for most zero order skills; failure to develop them marks one as an outcast. However, some are more important than others. For example, making your bed in an odd manner probably matters little but poor hygiene is very noticeable.

Going Through the Mountain
Many zero order skills are amenable to greater effort. For example, you can make lists of chores and tasks to complete and go through them in order each day. For hygiene, for example, one might make a list like this:

1. Shower, including hair wash
2. Dry self
3. Brush teeth, rinse and spit

4. Brush hair
5. Put on deodorant
6. Finish drying
7. Dress

The level of detail needed depends on how problematic these activities are for you. Some people will need no such list; others may need even more detail than this list has. In my morning routine, after my shower, I work "top-down"; first, I comb my hair, then take medicines, then shave, then apply deodorant. For many children "dress" will be much too broad.

Many activities of daily living are learned through practice; but one reason that NLDers may not improve as rapidly is related to the kinetic melodies mentioned earlier in this chapter (LaVoie, 1996).

Going Over the Mountain
Many zero order skills are also susceptible to taking more time. It matters little how long it takes to make the bed or brush your teeth, although time spent doing these things is time you can't spend doing something else.

Going Around the Mountain
To avoid making the bed, one technique is to get a sleeping bag, spread it on top of the bed, and, in the morning, simply roll it up and stick it under the bed. Another method is to use a futon or other type of bed where a "made" bed has nothing on it.

DECIDING AMONG THE OPTIONS
Although I think going around the mountain is often the best solution, each strategy has its place. You may realize, after trying other options, that some goals are not realistic for you, so giving up is

perfectly reasonable; indeed, giving up may be good option when you determine early on that the other options won't work. Conversely, some problems are so integral to your life that it may be wise to spend the effort and time to go through or around the mountain.

My advice is that, when you identify a problem caused by your NLD, you try to think of all the possible solutions from all the categories: giving up, going over, going through, and going around. To get help with listing your possibilities, ask friends and family or consult the resources I list on page 159. Once you have a list of possibilities, you can decide among them. Too often, we accept the first solution that comes to mind, even when it isn't optimal.

SOCIAL PROBLEMS
Many NLDers have social and emotional problems, but as Palombo (2005) points out, these are different in fundamental ways from those of people whose *primary* problem is social or emotional.

Many people with NLD have difficulty making friends. We NLDers can be gullible and too trusting, and we can have trouble transitioning between the levels of a relationship. That is, we may try to jump from casual acquaintance to deepest intimacy in ways that make others feel awkward. As mentioned, we have problems reading all the social cues that go along with language tone of voice, facial expression, body language, and so on. We have trouble telling good-natured teasing from meanness (Whitney, 2002) and discerning what things are told in confidence and which are open to share.

THE MOUNTAIN AND SOCIAL PROBLEMS

Giving Up on Social Problems
In social problems, the giving up results in withdrawal and in pretending we do not want friendship. This is a pretense. People

do vary in the degree to which they want friends, in how many friends they prefer, and in how much time they want to spend alone versus with other people. NLDers may want fewer friends and spend less time with friends than most people, but there are very few people who want no friends, and none of the NLDers I have met are among these few.

An extreme form of giving up on social problems is deliberately offending others in order to avoid the risk of rejection. Here, the rather silly saying that "you haven't failed unless you've tried" is stood on its head and becomes "if you haven't tried, you haven't really failed." I used this strategy in junior high school and the last years of elementary school. I did things I knew other kids would find offensive, so that, when they didn't want to be my friends, I could blame the offensive behavior and deflect attention from the notion that it might be *me* they didn't like. This wasn't a conscious strategy at the time, and it is ineffective. It fails to get you closer to your goal of having friends; to continue the mountain metaphor, it doesn't get you to the other side of the mountain (friendship) but lets you think you've avoided burial in a landslide (outright rejection).

A slightly less extreme form of this strategy is to pursue solitary interests. One such interest is reading, and many NLDers lose themselves in this activity for hours at a time. There is, of course, nothing wrong with reading, in and of itself. But if you want to make friends, spending time reading all day won't work.

Going Through the Mountain of Social Skills

Some exercises help with aspects of socialization. For paralanguage skills, it is useful to give examples of different tones of voice, volumes, nonverbal sounds, rates of speech and emphasis. In the next paragraph, I give roles to "teacher" and "student." This could be an actual student and teacher, or a parent and child, or an NLD adult and a friend or relative. Consider making it into a game.

Have teacher say the same sentence in a lot of different ways, and ask student to interpret. Then have student try to use tone, volume, nonverbal sounds, rates of speech, and emphasis to communicate different things. Teacher and student can watch TV shows together and try to identify different patterns. (This is especially useful if you record the show so it can be seen multiple times.) For a greater challenge, try watching a show that's in a language you don't speak. Another tool is to record student and then have teacher and student go over it together. Then have student try to make the sounds. Yet another idea is to watch videos of famous speeches, and see how the speaker uses nonverbal tools to increase the power of his or her speech.

For more exercises, see most any good book on NLD, e.g., the ones by Duke and Nowicki and their colleagues, or Lavoie (1996).

Going Over the Mountain of Social Skills

This entire area—paralanguage, facial expressions, space and touch, gestures and posture, rhythm and tone—is one where going over the mountain, that is, spending more time on a task, is simply not possible. All of these things happen in real time. You cannot, for example, ask someone to hold a certain facial expression until you "get it." You can't say to someone "just hold that expression a minute while I process what that combination of facial expression, body position, and tone means."

Indeed, one of the major problems of NLD is that we take time to process stuff that NT people process automatically and continuously. Even a delay in response can cost NLDers additional grief as misinterpretations are made of our hesitancy while we figure out an appropriate response.

Going Around the Mountain of Social Skills

Going around the mountain refers to finding alternate solutions. For social skills, the internet provides an enormous number of ways of getting around the mountain. Many, maybe most, of the difficulties we have with socialization disappear when we interact through type, rather than face-to-face. First of all, when communication is through type, there is no nonverbal communication: No faces, gestures are reduced to emoticons, or "smileys," no body language. You can't tell what clothes the person is wearing. The issue of body space disappears. Rhythm and tone shrink drastically in importance, although, in some media, it is possible to interrupt on the internet.

Another method, especially for children, is to choose friends who are either much younger or who are adults (Mamen, 2007).

Choosing Among the Options

Different people will find different combinations of these strategies useful. One tool that I find incredibly useful is the internet, for all the reasons I noted above. However, this depends in part with my being facile with words–not only am I verbal, but I am able to find the right word or response quickly. I can also organize my thoughts quickly. This, combined with adequate typing, lets online conversations flow easily. If you prefer a slower style of interaction, then reading and commenting on blogs may be best for you, since you will usually get far less interaction per minute than with a social media like Twitter. I mix this with a bit of the giving up strategies.

Other people may find the sorts of exercises referred to above more helpful than I do; this may be partly age-based—I am stuck in my ways at this point. A child or young adult may benefit much more from these exercises and may have more time to devote to them.

SENSORY OVERLOAD

Many NLDers have problems with sensory overload. This is partly because we have to process information consciously; something neuro-typical people do without thought. Sensory overload is more or less what it sounds like. There is so much coming at us via sight, sound, smell, touch that we become overwhelmed. Even people without learning disabilities can experience sensory overload—too many people, too many sights, sounds and smells at once. But we NLDers tend to have it more often, at lower levels.

THE MOUNTAIN AND SENSORY OVERLOAD

Giving Up on Sensory Overload

With regard to sensory overload problems, giving up would mean seeking to live with little input. How exactly this would play out would depend on the circumstances in which the overload arose. Thus, if the noise in restaurants or at parties overwhelms you, giving up would mean staying at home or engaging only in quiet activities. This is at least somewhat workable, but you'll miss a lot of socializing, and, if you are not careful in how you decline invitations, you may offend people. Also, there are some events you cannot avoid. But this is a case where giving up is not altogether ridiculous.

Similarly, if sights easily overwhelm you, it may be possible to arrange your living space and your workspace so that they are visually uncluttered. If, like many NLDers, you are driven mad by being in a dentist's chair, you could just wait for your teeth to fall out—this is not a good option. But you might find a sympathetic dentist and explain what bothers you and work out ways around it. One NLD child I know felt panicked by the chair moving. A way to help him is warning him when the chair is going up or down, or by letting him leave the chair while the dentist repositions it. (However, some dentists will refuse to listen; in this case, get a new dentist).

Going Through or Over the Mountain of Sensory Overload

"Trying harder" often makes overload problems worse. What is needed are ways to try less hard. There are also relatively few ways to take longer to deal with sensory overload. The problem is inherently happening all at once. If the input could be spread out, the problem would disappear.

Going Around the Mountain of Sensory Overload

Sensory overload manifests itself in various ways, and so there are various ways around the mountain. In lectures in school and in meetings at work, I find it difficult to look at a person and listen to them at the same time. I also find it hard to take notes, preferring to concentrate on listening. Therefore, I use my notepad for doodles. This makes it appear that I am taking notes (and thus not able to look at the speaker), freeing me to pay attention.

At home, when sensory overload overwhelms you, consider using one room as a refuge. As a child and adolescent, I found relief taking a long bath. Not only were baths calming in and of themselves (as they are for many people), but the bathroom is a spot where you are unlikely to be disturbed and where sensory input is limited. I also find it helpful to wake up early; early mornings tend to be quiet times. In a lot of cases, this is also a good strategy for work—more people stay late than come in early. (Take care that your boss knows you are arriving before everyone else.)

With excess noise, a straightforward solution is earplugs. However, consider the social situation. At a restaurant with friends, it would be unacceptably rude to put in earplugs.

However, if you are out with one very good friend, tell him or her about the problem, and ask that you use a pad to communicate (as if you were deaf and did not lip read) rather than talk out loud.

The earplug solution can work well in a workplace through a bit of subterfuge: wear them, pretending that they are playing music. If you buy a pair of earphones that are large, anyone wishing to talk to you will know you have them on and will give some sort of signal for you to take them off. Don't get the type that cancel all noise, as they block out things you need to hear (such as the phone ringing).

Similarly, in some situations, you can wear the sort of blindfold used for sleep, and I believe there are nose plugs that reduce smells.

Choosing Among the Options
Here there are really only two sorts of options: Going around or giving up. This difficulty is not one that affects me greatly, so I don't have a lot to suggest.

VISUAL-SPATIAL ORGANIZATION
Organization in every way is difficult for NLDers, from finding places to locating objects—like the glasses on my face!

THE MOUNTAIN AND SPATIAL ORGANIZATION

Giving Up on Spatial Organization
One can give up (to a degree) on spatial organization by minimizing one's possessions and then simply living in chaos. The problem is this approach tends to put off others when they see how you live, and it leads to misplacing stuff. Clearly, completely giving up is not a good option.

Going Through the Mountain of Spatial Organization

There are ways to try harder at spatial skills. A lot of these involve making lists or otherwise verbalizing what is involved. For example, if you have to get to a place that is unfamiliar to you, you could go to MapQuest on the Internet and type in the addresses of the starting and ending points to get written directions. Or, you could use a regular map and carefully write down the turns you have to take.

Going Over the Mountain of Spatial Organization

If you are willing to take longer than other people to do something, some organizational problems disappear. A benefit of being organized is that you become more efficient and can accomplish tasks more quickly. For example, one area where organization is important is getting ready for the day. Organization might mean fewer trips between rooms, less time looking for things, a quicker shower, and so on.

However, for some tasks, organization is highly important. For example, if you are the parent or caregiver of a baby, you need to figure out a way to change the baby's diapers safely. You cannot simply leave the baby on the changing table while you hunt for clothes, diapers, ointment, and wipes.

Going Around the Mountain of Spatial Organization

For spatial and organizational problems, there are a variety of methods of going around the mountain. Almost all NLDers have a very poor sense of direction, but some of us can use maps well. Many cities have features that make getting around a little easier. For instance, in Manhattan, on the cross streets, the odd numbers are always on the north side of the street and the even numbers on the south side. In Chicago, although the streets are named, they are all numbered from a central point, so that if you know the number north or south and the number east or west, you can find where you are going and tell how far away you are. But many cities are not even on a grid, and this can make getting around much harder for NLDers.

A tool that I and many other NLDers find useful is the smart phone. It's like a diary, address book, note pad, calculator, and more, all in one. Plus, it reminds me of things by beeping at me (if I set alarms). I back up the data on my smart phone onto my computer, so if I lose my phone, all I lose is money to purchase a new phone. (Unlike me, some NLDers dislike using the smart phone as an organizational tool.)

Other tasks yield to more particular solutions: For example, when I changed diapers on one of my kids, I did it on the floor. This could be messy, but it couldn't be disastrous. (A baby rolling on the floor might spread urine or feces, but the baby won't get hurt.)

Choosing Among the Options

Organization is a problem for almost every NLD person I know. The idea of "everything in its place" is inapplicable to us NLDers, because we cannot remember which thing goes in which place. We lose things, forget where they are, forget where we are, and forget where we are supposed to be and when. We have trouble organizing both space and time.

My own strategy here is to have a few key things that I always can locate. For example, I need to know where my glasses are. They are always either a) on my face, b) on my nightstand or c) on the sink in the bathroom (when I shower). I always keep my wallet in the same pocket or on my nightstand (when pants are in laundry). Each thing in only one of a few places. You could make a list of things that you have to be able to locate, and then figure a few spots where each of them can be. But don't try to do this with everything—overwhelming!

So, the key with regard to spatial organization may be to go through the mountain for key things, but give up on the mountain for other things, and around the mountain for yet others.

6: Baby to College

How does NLD manifest itself across the life span? Let's look at each stage and discuss typical problems that occur and coping strategies.

Early Childhood: Not Your Typical Baby

Early identification of NLD or some other LD is definitely helpful: the earlier an intervention starts, the more helpful it can be. However, an NLD identified early may suggest great severity. Although NLD is not an official diagnosis in the DSM-V and lacks a sanctioned list of symptoms or precursors, there are some unofficial anecdotal, early warning signs of NLD. Bear in mind that none of this is definitive. Any of these might be signs of NLD, or some other problem, or nothing at all.

Assessment

Prenatally, many NLDers move less than average. In early infancy, even immediately after birth, they may react atypically to stimuli, either over- or under-reacting. As noted in a previous chapter, they may reach traditional milestones (sitting, standing, walking, and toileting) later than usual. Nevertheless, early identification is difficult; in their comprehensive guide to young children with special needs, Howard et al do not mention nonverbal learning disabilities, nor do they mention Asperger's syndrome.

Around age 5, more assessments become available, but none that I know of are specific to NLD. Often, a professional who is evaluating an NLD child may know something is wrong, but either misdiagnoses it or, if he or she is perceptive, realizes that they do not know what it is. Although the situation is improving, many professionals do not know about NLD.

TYPICAL PROBLEMS

Mamen (2007) notes that the following are typical problems of NLD in young children:

- Avoidance of fine motor activities
- Problems with intelligibility of speech
- Difficulties with humor, analogy, symbolic language and other social uses of speech
- Less advanced social language, compared with use of vocabulary, syntax and so on
- Poor social interactions
- Hypersensitivity to stimuli
- Gross motor issues
- Coordination problems

Another problem she identifies is turn-taking. Babies start to learn turn-taking before they learn speech, but NLD children may show less of this skill than NT kids do.

COPING MECHANISMS FOR PARENTS

You've had a baby! Congratulations! Out of the hospital and home to the crazed life of new parents. And then…maybe early, maybe later, you realize, something is different about this baby. He isn't doing what his peers are doing. Or he's doing it differently. Or she's doing something they are *not* doing. Or something. Different. Your baby.

Off to books and websites and pediatricians and friends and... They all say different things!

- "It's a phase" (but this phase doesn't seem to end).
- "All kids are different" (but your kid, somehow, seems more different).
- "She'll outgrow it!" (Maybe. When?)
- If only you did something different it would be fine. (Such helpful advice!) It's *your* fault! (Thank you so much, helpful friend.)

Time passes and your baby is still *not* like other kids, in some way. And, one day, some expert or series of experts, gives... **a diagnosis**.

What's the first thing to do?

Well, as Douglas Adams said in *Hitchhiker's Guide to the Galaxy*: "DON'T PANIC."

Realize this: Your child didn't change when you heard the diagnosis. He has the same quirks and she has the same difficulties. But **you** changed.

- You gained information.
- You started along a path that may offer some help and support.
- You realized there are other kids who are like yours. (Even if your kid is 1 in a million, that means there are 7,000 people just like him).

Those are good things.

Later, there will be—trust me on this—many ups and downs. Good advice, bad advice, strange advice. But your child didn't change. You did.

LATER CHILDHOOD AND TWEENS — WHEN THE DEFECATION HITS THE VENTILATION

The later elementary grades is a typical time for NLD to get noticed. More and more complex demands are placed on children, both academically and socially. Many parents of NLDers say their children appeared fine until fourth or fifth grade. In some cases, it may be that the parents were in denial, and ignoring signs of trouble. In other cases, the signs are acknowledged, but are believed to be a phase. In yet other cases, the parents suspect that something serious is wrong, but are misled by experts who are unaware of NLD or unable to diagnose it. But sometimes the signs just aren't there.

ASSESSMENT

Tests that reveal NLD characteristics are not well-known and are unreliable for young children. The symptoms of NLD often appear to be other syndromes or to be "defiance" or "stubbornness." Certainly, children can be oppositional and stubborn. But NLD children frequently express complete confusion as to why they are being punished. It is like the joke about a family sitting around the dinner table when little Bobby says "Hey mom, could you please pass the f***ing potatoes?" Mom sends him to his room, admonishing him to think about how to behave at the dinner table. When he returns, she asks him what he wants. He says "I don't know what I want, but I sure as h*** don't want the f***ing potatoes!" Punishment, or any form of behavior modification, can only work if the child knows what behavior is being modified, and NLD children can be curiously obtuse about this recognition.

TYPICAL PROBLEMS

Friendships. By age 8 or 9 the NLD child's difficulty in forming friendships may become more obvious (and more painful).

Mamen (2007) suggests that social distance is related to physical distance; just as NLDers have problems with appropriate use of personal space, they may have difficulty negotiating among the levels of friendship: Acquaintance to casual friend to close friend to best friend.

KEEPING CONFIDENCES

Another difficulty that may surface is keeping secrets. It is not so much that the NLDer will deliberately tell secrets; rather, an NLDer may share a confidence (if not explicitly told to keep the information to himself).

COPING MECHANISMS

In education, this may be the time to start pursuing accommodations and an IEP (individualized education program), if you have not already done so. The details of an IEP vary depending on the needs of your child, but it might include a scribe (an aide who takes notes for the child) or alternate means of getting information from the teacher.

To help an NLD child, parents must carefully examine why certain behaviors are the way they are and explain them as well as possible to the child. How do you know that some things are said in confidence? How do you know how close to stand to another person? Explain these things in *words* and *rules*. "You and I can hug because I am your mom, but you don't hug people who are just friends except when X" and that sort of thing. Parents need to do their best giving explanations for social rules.

ADOLESCENCE: A FORM OF MENTAL ILLNESS?

Adolescence is a hard time of life for many people. For those of us who are "different" or "quirky" it can be agonizing, because the typical adolescent is desperate to fit in. NLDers crave belonging during adolescence, and their neuro-typical peers are eager to distinguish themselves from others by pointing out other teens' differences and making it clear that those differences are not good. Earlier in life, children are less aware of differences, and later in life, it is often possible to find people who are more accepting of differences.

In adolescence, you (if you go to a regular school) are forced to associate with all the NT adolescents. Later on, people tend to sort themselves into groups that may interact little with each other. High school is famous for cliques; these cliques are confined into single buildings, and often into single rooms. This is a recipe for problems.

Assessment

As children mature, assessment often becomes easier because more tests are available and there is a longer background of behavior to use in the assessment. If a child is seen for a psychological evaluation, the key thing is making sure the evaluators know that NLD exists (even if it is now part of autism spectrum disorder in the DSM-V).

Typical Problems

All of the earlier problems are exacerbated during adolescence. In addition, one's peers may learn to shift blame on the vulnerable or may use NLDers' desire for friends to get them to do things that are either against school rules or outright illegal. NLD children tend toward honesty according to Whitney and others researchers, but they are often gullible. So, if a sophisticated peer says, "Here, hold this and I'll be your friend," the NLDer may do it. Later, it may turn out that the item is stolen goods.

A less inimical problem that often arises in adolescence is being overly compliant with adult rules. Now, this may not seem like a problem to the adult! However, part of adolescence is rebellion against rules such as listening to music their parents can't stand and wearing clothes their parents find preposterous. Yet an NLD adolescent may still be wearing clothes picked out by his parents.

COPING MECHANISMS FOR PARENTS

There are some options for schooling and partial solutions for other problems. I urge parents to discuss these options with their adolescents (and I urge adolescents to discuss these options with their parents).

Also, some encouragement: You know that adolescence ends. Adolescents may know this fact intellectually, but they usually do not grasp it emotionally. When you were 14, didn't age 21 seem a long way off? It's half your life over again!

Parents need to try to tell their teens this in a roundabout way. Teens won't believe you if you tell them outright. Adolescents in general are not known for trusting adults (especially parents) and NLDers, although usually more trusting that NTers, may be even less wired for this sort of trust. But you can point it out subtly. You may use examples of things that happened when you were their age. (Do *not* use these as admonishments for their poor behavior, rather, as points of interest).

COLLEGE: BETTER DAYS!

For me, and for many NLDers, college is a great improvement over adolescence. You have more choices of classes and activities, and greater maturity. College kids want to stand out for their uniqueness; cliques are passé. All this benefits NLDers.

There are new challenges, as well. More organization is required. Some class assignments are long. Less supervision is given. The connection between amount of studying and grades is less immediate, and feedback may be more indirect.

ASSESSMENT

At this stage, many people self-assess; people become aware that they are having some sort of difficulty that is not caused by a lack of intelligence but by something else. They may then do their own research or may seek professional assessment.

TYPICAL PROBLEMS

While some problems may disappear in college, others surface. Lack of supervision in your dormitory or apartment may mean greater difficulty with daily living skills and with the lack of activities. Also, in the vast majority of college programs provide much less academic supervision than you had in high school. Many NLDers have problems with the organizational aspects of this. Finally, while in high school it was the duty of the school to provide accommodations (even if not all schools meet that duty all the time), in college it is not: It is your duty.

COPING MECHANISMS

Each person is unique, but I think that a small college can be better for people who need more accommodations in terms of test-taking, scheduling, and so on; larger schools may be better for people who are having social problems due to being "odd." While a small school may give more individual attention in academics, not social problems. With help for the social difficulties of NLDers, the advantages of the smaller school are minimized.

One way that college poses new challenges for the NLDer is in terms of accommodations and responsibility for advocacy. In high school, at least in theory, it is the school's responsibility to provide accommodations so that each child gets an appropriate education. In college, this is not the case. Even if a college is willing to accommodate students with learning disabilities (and this may not be so), it's the student's responsibility to get them.

This is good preparation for the work world, where there often are greater difficulties with getting accommodations. Indeed, I think that NLDers should use college as training for work and try to demand as few accommodations as possible while figuring out ways to accommodate on their own.

The accommodation that I think is most pernicious in this regard is also probably the most common one: Extra time. This is a relatively easy accommodation for a school to give. However, if you graduate from college having been given extra time on tests, then you will be in for a shock when you begin work, because, in the work world, this is a very hard accommodation to provide.

Of course, even this advice is not universal. Some people are slow at some things and fast at others, and you have to judge where you want to go with your life and what you will need to get there. Think through these three questions.

1. If you are slow at some task, is there a problem other than the task itself?
2. If you are slow, why you are slow at the particular task? For example, being slow at writing because of poor handwriting and graphomotor skills is different from being slow at writing because of problems with organizing your thoughts.
3. How that slowness may affect a career you're considering? Many skills taught in college are used in only certain careers, even in a given field. For example, if you major in the sciences, you may need to take laboratory courses, but by no means all science careers demand that set of skills. You will need to look at the various career possibilities in each field.

In fact, this same list could apply to any of your difficulties. Take poor handwriting. This is a big problem in school, but the accommodation might be allowing the NLDer to type or dictate answers on a test. But if the problem is speed of writing, then note-taking will be difficult; the accommodation might be for the student to take notes on a computer during class, to record the lecture (with the professor's permission), or to find a buddy who can take notes and share them with you, or to have a formal scribe assigned.

What are other accommodations? As always, a lot depends on the individual and his or her needs. Some possibilities are:

- Asking the professor if you can tape record lectures.
- Asking if you can audit a class prior to taking it for credit.
- Seeing if the professor can make his notes available.
- Finding a classmate to study with, or forming a study group.
- Finding out whether the professors make podcasts of their lectures.
- Finding a "bridge" or other assistance program formally offered by a college or other organization

Even with a lot of help, some people (both NLD and NT) may not succeed in formal schooling. Please be careful to not confuse failure at school with failure to learn. Indeed, the possibility of becoming self-taught, of being an autodidact, is strong. The disadvantage is obvious: One does not get a formal degree. But there are advantages too: First, it is much, much cheaper than formal university education; second, you set your own curriculum; and third, you can do it on your own schedule, taking as long as you want.

There have always been a lot of resources available to a would-be autodidact, and the Internet has expanded these enormously. Some of these are free, some are not. Some people may be willing to barter one sort of instruction for another.

Three of best known sites are:

MIT Open Coursware at http://ocw.mit.edu/index.htm.
Khan Academy at http://www.khanacademy.org
Coursera at http://www.coursera.org/

Before we visit adulthood in Chapter 11, including work, romantic relationships, and everything else, let's explore life with
NLD kids at home and at school.

7: Dealing with the NLD Child at Home

Parents can help their NLD child succeed by providing various at-home accommodations.

Quiet space. Many but not all people with NLD need time alone in a quiet space every day. To many of us, the world is overwhelming. So, if possible, home should have a space for the person to be alone. If a NLD child or adult can have a room alone, great. Not every family can do that. But it might be possible to have one room belong to the person for a certain period of each day.

Some people with NLD get easily overwhelmed by auditory or visual stimuli. Auditory stimuli can be blocked with noise-canceling earphones. But visual stimuli are not so easily blocked. So, if the NLDer in your home is easily overwhelmed visually, it would be good to have at least *some* space in the home that is visually calm—not a lot of stuff or clutter, not a lot of paintings, and so on.

Sensory stimulation. Different people prefer different levels of sensory stimulation; these ranges are often more extreme for NLD people, and the consequences of being at the wrong level are often more profound. Children may be highly sensitive to noise or to odors or to other stimuli. Others find high levels of stimuli relaxing. Or there may be combinations that don't seem to make sense, but work for the child (e.g., a child who doesn't mind loud noises but hates soft ones). Strong odors can be problematic for some NLDers. If you are cooking something that has a strong aroma, you may want to warn your child so she can play elsewhere in the house, or outside, or provide for more ventilation.

Touch. Another thing that can overwhelm NLDers is physical proximity and touch; I think some of us have visual processing issues that make it harder for us to keep track of who is where and what might happen. One way to deal with this would be to set up some guidelines for how to touch your NLDer.

Use words, words, words. Another sort of accommodation is part of everyday life: Explain why in words. Use words a lot. Use them even when you think what you are saying is obvious, because to the NLD child, it may not be. This can also affect punishment: Punishment when the child does not understand why he is being punished is not only ineffective, it's torture.

Verbal explanations can cover a lot of ground. For example, Whitney (2002) notes that her son accepted reasons to comb his hair such as, "If you comb it that way, people will think you are goofy." NT kids figure out the proper way to comb their hair by looking at other kids; NLD kids may not. A separate issue is what to do (with an NT or NLD child) when the kid *wants* to look goofy. This is something that will depend on your parenting style, the particular issue, and the age of the child. It's one thing to rebel on purpose; it's another to rebel without knowing it.

Routines and planning. Routines are very important to most NLD people, and changes in routines should, whenever possible, be planned and the child told what to expect. But the child may *still* be upset by the change in routine, so you should also plan for that. Of course, you can't always do this whenever possible, you should.

Another, related topic is planning. Suppose there is a party you have to go to as a family. Parties are very stressful for many

NLDers. They involve overwhelming sensory input and change to routine. So, plan. If you can, plan an escape route–a way out of the party in case of meltdown. If that isn't possible, try to plan a safe place for your NLDer to retreat to; and let your hosts know of your concerns–after all, they don't want a meltdown either! Another aspect of planning is scheduling. Many NLDers do well with schedules; at first, the schedule may have to be written (one good way is to write it on a whiteboard that can be kept visible) but it may eventually become routine. It's when our routines are changed that problems occur!

HOLIDAYS AND THE NLD CHILD

Holidays can be a lot of fun but they can also be stressful even for the most neuro-typical (NT) people. Routines are altered. Often, we are visiting family or friends or they are visiting us. Many meals are different than usual. Schools are closed. People have days off. Things are **different**.

For most people these differences and this stress are worth it for the joys that holidays bring. But many NLD people have more trouble than most with changes in routine. How can we help our children or ourselves deal with this?

The sources of stress. What makes the holidays so stressful for NLD people? Change! Change is hard. NLD children are used to their parents and their parents are used to them. Maybe not always as accepting or cherishing as they might be, but at least familiar. NLD adults have often adapted their environments to suit themselves. Other family members and friends will be less familiar and (often) less accepting. This places added stress on all.

What can you do? Here are some suggestions:

- Prepare your "others." If you are visiting relatives or they are visiting you, tell them about your child ahead of time.

Try to anticipate ways that your child may behave in ways that are unusual or irritating. That won't make them less unusual or irritating, but at least people are prepared.

- Prepare your NLDer. Many NLD people hate changes in routine but deal with them better if they are anticipated. So, tell your child, as precisely as possible, what will happen when. "On Tuesday we will wake up early to go to the airport. There will be lines. The flight may be crowded or delayed. It should last about two hours. Then we will visit Uncle Bill for three days. They live in a house that…" and so on.

- Give your child "outs." Maybe your family likes to spend hours around the dinner table on a holiday. Your NLD child probably doesn't. Forcing him or her to do so is a route to disaster. So, arrange ways he or she can avoid change. A room he can go to when he's done eating works well. This may take planning. Or, if you are planning many meals out, maybe leave your kid home for some of them (with appropriate supervision, of course!) A dinner of mac and cheese in front of the TV can be very nice.

- Avoid the worst "others." Some people just don't get it. Unfortunately, some of these people are our friends and relatives. So, if possible, avoid those people. Or, perhaps, keep your interactions with these people separate from your interactions with your kid.

ANXIETY? YEAH!

So, a lot of people with LD or autism or Asperger's or whatnot are **anxious**. Some are so anxious it's a disorder. Maybe we're born with it. Maybe it's given to us.

Because, for many people with LD or autism or Asperger's or whatnot, the world keeps tossing us the unexpected. Praise for what's easy. No praise for what's hard. Blame for God knows what (yeah, it's obvious to you, if you're neurotypical, but it's not obvious to us! What did we do wrong? What did you want? What did you want us to do? What did you do? How should we know that?)

And then, blango! Out of the blue: YOU GOT IT WRONG!

Here's another important suggestion:

A key role of parents and teachers is to give children (NLD or not) tasks that are at the appropriate level of difficulty and to praise and correct appropriately. Bear in mind that praise should be given for effort as well as for results, but that what requires effort may be quite different for an NLD child than an NT one. As a child, I frequently got praise for things that were easy for me, and no praise for things that were difficult. Not only did this not improve my sense of self-worth or motivate me to greater effort at the things that were hard for me, it also made me regard adults' words as worthless and as things to be ignored.

After a while of random punishments and rewards for no apparent reason we get **anxious**. If you do that to rats, they get anxious. If you do it to dogs, they get anxious. If we didn't, we'd have to be catatonic.

A Safe Place

It is vitally important that all people have a safe place. This is especially so for LD people, who may experience the world as less safe than most people do. A safe place is one where the person is safe from physical *and emotional* harm.

For many LD people, the world is harsh. People can be intentionally cruel, they can also be unintentionally cruel. The former would be when a person is teased or bullied (either in person or via the Internet). Both can occur in other situations as well. A safe place is free from these dangers.

In addition, a disabled person (LD or physical disability) is unable to do easily some things that normal people can do easily. He or she may be unable to do it at all; or it may simply require more effort. Both are exhausting, emotionally. A safe place is one where this difficulty is minimized, as well.

The exact nature of safety will vary from person to person as well; for a blind person, safety would perhaps concentrate on the physical nature of the space, and the sameness of the placement of physical objects. If a blind person knows exactly where things are, then he or she can navigate that space more comfortably and with less effort, and with much less risk of tripping, banging or breaking. For some LD people, safety will involve a lack of noise. For others, it will involve minimal visual distractions. But for all, it will involve emotional safety.

What can a safe place be for a child? For some, it can be home. For a child, if the parents set up the home so that it is safe, and are emotionally safe for their child, then the home can be a safe place. But this requires a special set of abilities and efforts on the part of the parents. If there are other children in the family, this may make it harder, as parents devote time to their other children (and to themselves!). No parents are superhuman; and some are, themselves, troubled with issues that make it hard for them to provide safety to others.

If the entire home cannot be made safe, it may be possible to make one portion of it a safe place. However, some parents may be unable, for various reasons, to make any part of the home really safe. In this case, it may be necessary to find some alternative place. This can take a variety of forms. It could be a therapist's office, a relative's home, or the home of a close friend of the family or of the child. There are lots of possibilities.

Or a safe place could be something else entirely, depending on what disability is involved. It could involve:

- A particular kind of lighting
- Neatness
- Control of position (that is, whether you are standing or sitting or lying down, and in what particular position)
- Quiet
- Noise
- Available care and communication

But without a safe place, the person must be constantly on guard against all the many dangers of the world. That's a horrible way to grow up and a horrible way to live; it stultifies and damages, and prevents growth.

SIBLINGS AND THE NLD CHILD

Siblings can be vitally important to an NLD child (or adult). They can be a great support or a great hindrance. Mine were a great help. I got lucky. One of the ways I got lucky is that they think *they* got lucky.

My sister (technically, my half-sister, but we have an unhyphenated relationship) was 12 when I was born. She was an enormously competent 12 year old—so much so that our mother trusted her to take care of me. Once, when I was a baby, she took me to the park and was pushing me in a swing. A woman came up to her and said "WHAT are you DOING with that BABY!?" and my sister turned to her and said "that baby is my brother, and I am ENTERTAINING him." (And I can easily see her doing this.)

Eighteen months after I was born, my brother came along. I was an odd-looking, skinny, cranky, strange-acting child. My brother was a blue-eyed, blond-haired, chubby-cheeked cutie. So, everyone oohed and aahed even more over the new baby than usual. My sister decided she was having none of that! No! *I* was the one. Until a couple months when she told our parents that she couldn't help liking our brother because "he makes himself so charming." But, nevertheless, I've always been closer to my sister than my brother has.

So, there I am, this messed up little baby with this adorable brother. Recipe for...a great relationship. It's weird how these things work out sometimes. My brother and I shared a room until I was about 15. For most of that time, it was by choice. In the apartment where we spent our tweens and teens, there were two rooms for us. But, until I was 15, we shared one as a bedroom and used the other for other stuff.

And, even after I decided I wanted my own room, we did a lot together. I helped him with his homework. (Yeah, my dysfunctional brain is good at some stuff, like math and writing). He provided relationships, because I had no friends from sixth to eleventh grades. None. I think I had one date (and that was a disaster) and I don't recall any "play dates." But my brother had tons of friends. He loved being around people. And people loved being around him, too. He made himself charming. And I got to share.

Meanwhile, my sister had gone off to college (but she came home some) and then got married. She lived for a little while in Lawrence, Kansas, but for most of the time she lived in Chicago. I used to go visit. A lot. Several times a year. Because it was just a lot easier being in her house than being in my parents' house. How many people go to Chicago for Christmas vacation?

So, even though for a lot of kids in the autism ballpark, sibling relationships are really difficult, for me they were good. Why? Well, Calvin Trillin was once asked the secret to his long, happy marriage. He said "I walked into the right party." That's how I feel. I got lucky. That's not much help to others, I guess. I don't know how my brother and sister decided to put up with me. But I'm really glad they did.

TELEVISION

Television gets a bad rap and some of that is deserved; it can be a form of mindless entertainment, and I certainly wouldn't advocate a huge amount per day. However, as Whitney (2002) points out, it can also be a tool for learning. First, it can be part of the downtime that many NLDers need. Many shows can be lessons in social behavior (either as good advice or bad). Also, trying to guess the emotions on the actors' faces and voices can be a useful exercise.

GAMING

Another activity that often gets negative press is gaming, especially online gaming. It is possible to overdo gaming and even become addicted to it. However, it, too, is not all bad. The newer "social" games offer people an opportunity to socialize in a way that is constrained and centered. It is constrained by the use of text exclusively (unless you are making videos of yourself) and it is centered on a particular game. This has advantages for NLD people. When I was a child I played a lot of chess even though I wasn't very good. It gave me a way to socialize.

One question to ask is whether the gaming is a replacement for in-person social interactions. Gaming is fine as long as it is in addition to regular, in-person interactions.

WHEN THINGS GO WRONG

When things go wrong—and they will—the first thing to do (if necessary) is for the NLDer to reach calmness and let things settle down. But then you can use what went wrong to help prevent it going wrong again. And the way to do this is to break things down into smaller tasks. A parent or other helpful adult can help with this.

Sometimes it may mystify the parent of an NLD child—who in other areas is so bright—is having trouble with a task. So break it down. If your child has trouble dressing, put it in small steps: If "First underwear, then pants" isn't enough, then you may need to say "put one leg in each hole in the underwear, pull the underwear up so that the waistband is above your hips but below your belly button." Some people need this level of specificity. And the same logic applies to activities from brushing your teeth to taking an air plane ride: Break it down into small steps.

Also, when *you* do something wrong (and you will, no matter how hard you try; you're not perfect), it is key to apologize to your NLD child. An apology is seen by some as a sign of weakness; I see it as a sign of strength. Being strong enough to admit you were wrong is a good thing. In addition, if your child hears you apologize (and not be demeaned, fall apart, or anything) then she may be more ready to apologize when she does something wrong.

8: Education and the Mountain

MANY NLDERS HAVE FEW ACADEMIC PROBLEMS. THOSE THAT DO tend to have problems in a few areas:

- Graphomotor problems—poor handwriting, which can lead to illegible answers, or to arithmetic errors from misreading our own writing, or from teachers misreading our writing.
- Speed of processing problems are especially problematic on timed tests, where many NLDers have difficulty finishing on time.
- Problems in some areas of mathematics, especially those that require abstract thinking, more particularly abstract visual thinking, such as in geometry and some applications of calculus.

Problems in school may also arise due to distractibility or difficulty dealing with complex sensory input. Some of this can be avoided through various accommodations. One such is preferential seating: If a child is distracted by looking at other children, seating her in the front row may help. Children may also develop self-soothing methods. These should be discouraged only if they disturb others. Help the child find other soothing behaviors that are less disturbing.

THE MOUNTAIN MANIFESTED: ACADEMICS

GIVING UP

Giving up on academics is straightforward: Drop out of school.

Unfortunately, dropping out of school poses problems for future employment. The jobs that do not demand much academic education are ones that NLDers are typically bad at (e.g., waiter/ waitress, supermarket worker, some kinds of sales jobs, acting, construction worker, and so on). They often demand physical coordination and speed, or, in the case of sales, rapidly sensing what another person is feeling, and forming bonds with others quickly. Fortunately, many NLDers actually like school and do fairly well at it (although some may need various accommodations). Giving up before graduating high school is a last resort.

GOING THROUGH THE MOUNTAIN

In academics, working *harder* is usually equated with working *longer*, but there are differences. Working harder (going through the mountain) could involve working with fewer distractions (e.g., turning off the TV and radio; not multi-tasking while studying). This strategy may pay bigger dividends for some NLDers than for our NT peers; that is, the gains from eliminating distractions may be larger for us.

If it is not possible to arrange your living quarters to eliminate distractions, then it may be possible to study in the school library (particularly in high school or college) or at a public library. Many people study at Starbucks and other coffee shops—the level of noise varies, but at least the noise is not directed at you personally.

Another alternative for those with noisy homes is to study early in the morning or late at night, when things tend to be quieter; but you still need to be careful to get sleep, so this strategy is tricky to implement.

GOING OVER THE MOUNTAIN

This is probably the area where going over the mountain is most recommended; it may also be the area where it is most useful: study more. It may not be fun, it may not be desirable, but many successful NLDers found it worked! This strategy can be combined other ideas— use your ingenuity.

GOING AROUND THE MOUNTAIN

Ways of going around the mountain of academics vary by subject

Math

Mathematics offers tremendous opportunities for going around the mountain.

Math is often listed as an area that NLD children have difficulty. Rourke (1995) said that difficulty with math, especially abstract math, is a characteristic of NLD. I think this difficulty may be due to reliance on visualization in teaching mathematics. Most neuro-typical children (and adults) do best when math is taught in this way, and there is a correlation between spatial ability and math ability. But the correlation is far from perfect. I am good at math, but I think about it non-visually.

Some people with NLD may also have dyscalculia—that is, a learning disability about math to the extent that they have trouble learning even the most basic math, such as counting, one-to-one correspondence, or the relative size of objects. However, for most NLDers, math starts causing problems when concepts become more abstract; the difficulties seem to begin in fourth grade when word problems are introduced, and other math problems start requiring multiple steps.

In any case, the difficulties of math for NLDers are usually related to visualization. An example: suppose you ask a child how many forks will be needed when the family sits down to dinner.

A neuro-typical child may have no trouble visualizing his family, visualizing forks, and matching them up. But an NLD child may have trouble with these visualization tasks. A solution may be for him to count the family by name; or even order them by age and then count.

Here are other math helps:

Multiplication table. You learn it by rote (which some, but by no means all, NLDers seem to be good at) or you can learn tricks. I hated rote memory work, so I devised a lot of tricks, as follows.

2 times ____ is one that few people seem to have trouble with. One way of doing it, though, is to just add the number to itself.

3 times ____ is another that a lot of people just get. But you can add the number to twice the number. For example: Well, twice 8 is 16, and 8 more. You can partially check your answer by adding the digits in the answer and seeing if it is a multiple of 3. (For example, with 24, we add 2 and 4, to get 6, which is a multiple of 3.)

4 times ____ is just twice twice.

5 times ____ If you feel comfortable dividing by 2 (cutting in half) then you can add a 0 and then divide by 2 (e.g., add a 0 to 7 to get 70. Cut in half to get 35). If you don't like cutting big numbers in half, you can cut the original number in half, rounding down, and then add a 5 if you needed to round (e.g., cut 7 in half and round down to get 3, add a 5 (because you had to round) to get 35.

9 times ___ (Yes, I know I skipped 6, 7, and 8, I'm coming back to 8, and will talk about 6 and 7). There are several tricks for 9. Here are two I like:

° *The finger trick.* Hold out your hands, fingers spread and pointed up, palms away from you. Your left pinky is finger number 1, your left ring finger is finger 2, and so on. To multiply a number by 9, hold down the corresponding finger. Then, the tens digit is the number of fingers to the left, and the units digit is the number of fingers to the right. For example: Finger 6 is your right thumb. Fold it down, and there are five fingers to the left and four to the right, so the answer is 54.

° *Then subtract 1 then subtract from 9 trick.* To multiply by 9, subtract one from the number you want to multiply, that's the tens digit. Then subtract that number from 9, and that's your units digit. For example, with 7 times 9, first subtract 1 from 7. This equals 6. Now subtract 6 from 9. This equals 3. So the answer is 63.

8 times___ Multiply by 9, then subtract the number that you are multiplying.

6 and 7 times ___ OK, I admit it. I don't have tricks for these. But that only leaves three multiplication facts to learn, and you can probably manage that.

Estimation. Estimation involves getting a quick idea of the approximate answer. For example, in a multiplication problem, the number of digits in the answer is always either the sum of the number of digits in the two multiplicands, or one less than that. This is more clearly shown in an example. Suppose, for instance, the problem is 342*32. Well, 342 has 3 digits, and 32 has two digits, so the answer must have either 5 digits or one less that that (4 digits). If you have a long division problem, this method can be used to check if your answer is possible.

Digit checking. Digit checking means that certain final digits are possible. For example, in the above problem (342*32) the final digit of the answer must be 8; for another example, if the problem is 3456*789, you can tell that the answer must have either 6 digits or 7; and the last digit must be 4. Quite a variety of digit checks exist. For example, if the problem involves squaring a number, the last digit must be 0, 1, 4, 5, 6, or 9.

Divisibility tricks. One number is divisible by another if a dividing one by the other leaves no remainder. Divisibility by 3 (and 9) can be checked by adding up the digits and seeing if the result is divisible by 3 (e.g., 4643 cannot be the result of multiplying an integer by 3 (or 9), because which is not divisible by 3. A number is divisible by 4 if, and only if, the last 2 digits of the number are divisible by 4 (e.g 4,222,312,148 is divisible by 4 because 48 is). Similarly, a number is divisible by 8 only if the last 3 digits are (so the number above is not divisible by 8, because 148 is not). A number is divisible by 5 if the last digit is 0 or 5, and a number is divisible by 6 if it is divisible by 3 and it is even. I know of no simple divisibility trick for 7.

Science

NLDers often have a lot of trouble with the laboratory parts of some sciences, due to our poor visual-spatial abilities and our lack of coordination. One way around this mountain is to try to find someone who does well at the laboratory parts of science, but may not excel with the theory, and see if you can be partners. Since many NLDers are good at writing, it might be that one partner could do the experiments while the other writes it up. (Be sure to OK this with your teacher).

History/Social Studies

One aspect of history that may cause particular difficulties for NLD children is the temporal flow of history and getting a sense of when things happened. Part of this is alleviated by dates. Also, whereas NTers get a lot from the context of history NLDers may have more trouble with this. This is one thing that gets harder in the higher grades and in college; the student is expected to abstract more from a passage rather than rely on explicitly given information. At its simplest level, this could be inferring that people die after they are born; but on higher levels we have to infer that things happening in one place and time must have happened after those in another place. One problem I have when reading history (not textbooks, but general nonfiction) is remembering what year it is at any given point in the narrative.

English/Literature

NLDers are often facile readers, at least as far as vocabulary and knowledge of grammar go; they may have more problems with the more abstract aspects of fiction—especially the visual aspects, which are much more prevalent than you may realize. They may also have trouble "getting" the mores of particular eras from subtle cues.

For example, descriptions of clothing, and description of people's faces, expressions and tones of voice may convey less to the NLDer than to neuro-typical people. This problem may be more evident with "better" literature. One piece of advice given to fiction writers is "show, don't tell" but NLDers often need to be told about these things.

Expository Writing

Many NLD people have trouble with writing, especially with the longer essays that are required in high school and college. It's usually not so much the writing itself as the organization that causes problems. One method that I have found useful is what I call super-outlining. Start with a main topic. This might be assigned by the teacher, or it might be your choice. It could also be a limited choice for instance, you might be required to write an essay about one of the U.S. presidents in the 20th century, but have a choice about which.

Once you have a main topic, you make sections and write a bit (say, a paragraph or two) about each. For a short essay, that might be enough. If not, divide each section into subsections, and write about each of them. Keep going until your essay is about the right length, then fix the format and punctuation, work on the flow between sections, and you are done. A very long work might have many levels.

One approach to writing that is often helpful with people who are dyslexic is, in my experience, contraindicated for NLDers: Graphic organizers. These attempt to let the student put different ideas in different types of boxes and use other kinds of visual aids to writing. This is exactly the opposite of what NLDers need.

Foreign languages

I was never very good at foreign languages. I studied Spanish in high school, and, much later, lived in Israel and studied Hebrew. I have a couple hints for NLD students of foreign languages, based on my own experience and that of others:

- Don't try to learn a language with another script.
- When learning vocabulary, try to come up with cognates (words that sound similar and have similar meanings).

If I were learning Spanish now, I would list vocabulary in three columns: Spanish, English, and Cognate. This is easy with the Romance languages, particularly if, like many NLDers, you know English well. For example, the Spanish for "Earth" is "Terra," which doesn't seem to be a cognate, but there are words like "terrarium" and "terrestrial."

TYPE OF SCHOOL

SPECIAL EDUCATION VS. MAINSTREAM VS. HOME

Since this book is mainly about teenagers and adults with NLD, in most cases, this decision will already have been made, and the readers of this book will be coping with the aftermath of the choice.

My own view on special education is quite positive. As I noted in the Preface, my mother started a special education school for me, and I served on the board of that school, and my son attended it. Back when she was starting the school, she held lots of meetings with potential parents.

One mother said that she did not want her son to attend such a place, because he would not be considered "normal." Mrs. Napier-White, who my mother describes as a very proper Victorian lady, turned to this woman and said, "I don't like normal people. I never have."

While it is true that a "label" from a special education school can follow a child, I think this may be less of a problem than many seem to think it is. Children graduate from special education all the time and have been doing so for decades. Some of students never leave special education, but others (me, for example) go on to successful academic lives.

There is still a stigma attached to having attended a special school, but this seems to be lessening. Besides, the important thing to your child would be better off with a label that comes from a special education school or with a derogatory one given by peers in a regular school.

An alternative to a special school or a regular school is home-schooling. Home-schooling is increasingly popular in the United States. For some, it may be a temporary solution to an undesirable school placement; for others, it is a commitment throughout the school years.

The Mainstream: Where Fish Drown

It's so enticing. The mainstream. Maybe our children aren't so different, so unusual. Maybe they are "normal." Maybe they belong in the mainstream. But maybe not. Maybe parents' goal ought not be a mainstream **education** for their children but a mainstream **life**? After all, we will spend about 12 years in elementary and high school, and, if we live to be 80, we will spend about 62 years in our post-high school life.

I know I would have drowned in the mainstream as an elementary school student, and I nearly drowned in the mainstream for junior high school and high school. After that, things got better, and I am doing OK in the mainstream adult world. But I am fairly sure I would have done better had I been in special education longer.

One thing we shouldn't forget about mainstream education is that it's a lot cheaper than special education; and state bureaucrats love to save money. The bureaucrats aren't evil people–they've been told what to do. Budgets are being cut. Money must be saved. And a law saying we should all be in "least restrictive environments" sells a lot better than one that says we should be in "the least expensive environments." How often does the least restrictive environment serve the best interest of the child and the adult that child will become? Not as often as some would like to think.

And the "least restrictive environment" is often planned in one way, and then carried out in another. Plans are laid for highly skilled aides, then the budget axe falls again. There are less skilled aides. Or no aides. And the classes get bigger, and teachers get even more overworked.

Some fish can swim in the mainstream; but some can't.

LARGE VS. SMALL VS. HOME

When trying to find a good school for a child with NLD, one decision is mainstream versus special education. I talked about that above. But another decision, particularly if you decide against special education, is the size of the school. Clearly, schools vary in size across a huge range, but we can talk, in general, about big schools and small schools. Then there's the smallest school of all: Home school.

Each of these will be right for different children or even for the same child at different ages. Here are my thoughts on the advantages and disadvantages of each.

Small schools are probably what comes first to mind when considering a placement. The advantages are fairly clear: Your child may receive more individual attention; a higher proportion of the staff will know your child well; any problems that arise may be identified more quickly. The disadvantages may be less obvious, at least to people who are not themselves LD or not expert in LD: Individual attention may also come from other children (and in unwelcome ways). Your child may become "the weird one." NLD children (and other children in the autism ballpark) often have unusual interests; in a small school, it will be less likely that other children share those interests.

Large schools have almost opposite advantages and disadvantages. If the school is not very well run, your child may fall between the cracks and be ignored. On the other hand, in a large student body there will be more children who are comparable to your child, both in terms of disabilities and interests.

Then there's home school. I know relatively about this, but it seems to me to offer some unique advantages and disadvantages. The biggest advantages would be knowledge of your child and flexibility of program. The disadvantages (in addition to practical issues of cost and finding materials and instructors) would be making and keeping friends.

None of these advantages and disadvantages are set in stone. There are good big schools that manage to track every child well; there are small schools that make huge efforts to find a cohort for each child; and homeschooling can work very well, as well.

9: Teachers—
Don't Freak Out

NOTE: THIS CHAPTER STANDS SOMEWHAT APART FROM THE REST of the book, and each section stands on its own as well; I hope that teachers find it particularly helpful.

So, you're teaching. Good for you. Teachers are wonderful; the vast majority work very hard and care a lot about the kids they work with. But no one is perfect and...there's this kid in your class who is driving you CRAAAAZY!

Maybe this kid has an IEP, maybe not. Maybe she has an official diagnosis, maybe not. If this kid was in your school last year, maybe you've heard about him, maybe not. But whatever, the kid is driving you nuts. He seems to care about school–at least sometimes. She doesn't seem like a "bad" kid but she's always getting in trouble. Maybe he says he has a learning disability, but he doesn't seem bad at math or reading–or maybe she seems awful at math, but that isn't the problem that's making you nuts; you know how to help kids with math. But something is...off about the kid.

Quite possibly the child has nonverbal learning disorder. Quite possibly she is not picking up the nonverbal cues that you are giving subconsciously (or maybe consciously)–things like body language, tone of voice, facial expression, and volume. But just as some kids don't learn to read the usual way (we call these kids dyslexic) or who don't learn to do math the usual way (we

can them dyscalculic) or who can't sit still for as long as most kids
(ADHD), there are some who don't learn to read these nonverbal
cues—and they are said to have nonverbal learning disorder (NLD)
(if you are reading this book, you probably at least suspect this).
I hope this book has some good hints for you; please also check
out my website which is full of articles about this disorder and
these kids. The nice thing about my site is that Iif youask questions, I will try to answer. There are ways to reach these kids. Go
to www.IAmLearningDisabled.com.

Don't freak out!

How To Decrease Agitation for Some NLD Students

You're teaching. One of your students, you think, has nonverbal
learning disabilities. He's getting upset. With other kids, you
have lots of tools in your arsenal; things you know by instinct or
from training or from other teachers. But, with this kid, some
of those tools don't seem to work. What might work?

With many NLD kids, in many situations, agitation comes
from too much stimulation. So you want to decrease the amount
of stimulation the kid is getting. How you could do this will depend on your classroom, the age of the child, how agitated he is
and so on, but here are some ideas.

Some of these require advance planning. But, as Gail Godwin
said "Good teaching is one-fourth preparation and three-fourths
theater."

- You could move his chair to a quieter part of the room.
- You could send him on an errand ("Could you bring these
  to the main office?").
- Divide your room into smaller groups.
- If your class ever watches movies, this might be good.
- You could have a "step out" room or place, where a student

can go to be alone for a bit. (Be sure not to make this punitive.)

- Some NLD people (and people in the autism ballpark) are soothed by repetitive motions, sometimes called "stims." Work with the student to find one that doesn't disturb others.
- Deep breathing and other calming methods that work for NT people often work with NLD people as well. Get the kid to take a breath!
- Visualizing a calm place. Work with the kid separately to identify a scene or situation she finds calming
- Other NLD people report that physical activity, especially things like pushing against a wall, are calming.
- More general solutions could include headphones that block out some noise; also, many NLD people find music soothing.

Doubtless you can come up with others and you have to pick something that will work for this kid in this situation.

COMMUNICATING WITH NLD KIDS

Sometimes communication with that NLD kid just doesn't seem to work. What might you try?

Write. People with NLD have problems with many of the nonverbal aspects of communication. When you speak, you use these, often unconsciously. And you expect your listener to get the information, even if you don't realize you expect it. That's why many people prefer the phone to e-mail and in-person to either: They allow nonverbal communication. But your student may not be getting it. On the other hand, many NLDers are very good at the strictly verbal parts of language.

1. *Be specific.* This is probably good advice when communicating with any student, but it's especially so for NLD people. If your assignment is, "Write an essay" then you may expect the kids to realize what you want (based on grade level, amount of time, previous assignments and so on). NLD may not know what to do. Give specifics like long the essay should be and whether to use references.

2. *Communicate one-on-one.* One area that many people with NLD have trouble with is communication in groups. If you are talking and some other kids are talking and another group of kids is doing something else... it's easy for NLDers to lose track. Also, if you need to say something important to your NLD student, communicate when the two of you are separated from the group.

3. *Check.* Check if the student understood your communication. It's best to check right after you have communicated than to wait and see.

4. *Use e-mail.* E-mail can be very effective, because it can be saved, read at leisure, read more than once. And you can point to it later.

5. *Encourage feedback.* Almost no one wants to say "I don't understand". But you can make it a little easier for kids to say this by arranging ways for them to say it to you privately.

6. *Avoid words like "clearly," and "obviously."* If what you are saying is clear to the student, then he or she knows it is clear. And if it is not clear, then you've just made the student feel stupid (and less likely to communicate).

7. *Last but not at all least, use words.* Use words even when things are obvious (to you). Pretend you are texting and don't rely on nonverbal cues.

BREAK THINGS DOWN

Maybe you think this isn't necessary: You're a teacher, you already know to break things down. Indeed you do, when it comes to things like reading or math or art or gym. But what about how to stand in line or how to make a friend? These are tasks some NLDers have problems with. They, too, can be broken down into steps. You, as an NT teacher, may even know better than I how to do this breaking down; you just need to be aware that it is necessary.

DISCIPLINE MATTERS

A classroom needs to be ordered. Keeping a classroom ordered often requires discipline of students. Disciplining students with NLD is trickier than disciplining NT kids because NLD kids may not realize what they are doing wrong.

One young NLDer (see Whitney, 2002) thought he was being send to the principal's office for scratching his sock. Be explicit. If a child doesn't know what you are upset about then:

a) The child can't stop, even if he wants to, and;
b) You aren't disciplining the child, you are torturing him.

It may be obvious to you what the child is doing wrong. It may be obvious to most other kids that age. But it may not be remotely obvious to the child.

NO GROUP ASSIGNMENTS

Group assignments can be wonderful for NT kids; they may be especially wonderful for kids with language-based LD, as they can use their strengths. But for NLD kids, they can be disastrous since the NLD child does not know how to negotiate the group.

SEEING THE INVISIBLE—A GUIDE FOR TEACHERS

Disabilities come in different forms. Some are visible. If a person is in a wheelchair, you can tell. Some disabilities are invisible. NLD is doubly invisible.

Here are questions to ask yourself about the student who is off in some way. They may point to NLD.

Do you have a child in your class who looks like he was dressed by his mom at an age when all the other kids dress in ways that offend their moms?

Do you have a child who never seems to have any friends, but you can't see why?

Do you have a child who covers her ears at loud noises? Or soft noises?

Do you have a child who doesn't quite have ADHD exactly, but who seems to be off somewhere, distracted by things going on in his own head?

How about one who gets lost trying to find the classroom? Or can't figure out how to unlock a locker?

Do you have a student that fits a few of the above? Then you've seen the invisible. No one can diagnose an LD based on a single behavior or two; but these are among the warning signs. These signs alert you to the autism/NLD/Asperger's ballpark.

TEN THINGS WE WISH OUR TEACHERS KNEW

For a teacher, a child with NLD can be a puzzle. I am sure I was a puzzle to my teachers! Here are some things I wish they had known:

1. Just because I'm disabled doesn't mean I'm not abled.
    There are things I can do badly, there are things I can
    do well and there are some things I can't do at all. If you
    help me use what I am good at to do what I am bad at,
    things will go more smoothly for both of us.

2. I often need instructions in a different way; this
    doesn't mean I can't learn. Some kids learn better by
    listening, some by reading, some by watching someone
    do something. Don't assume that I am not interested in
    learning just because your instructions didn't seem to
    take; I might need them in a different format. Once I've
    figured out the instructions, I can learn a lot of things.

3. You can ask me questions. If you notice that I'm not do-
    ing what you think I should be doing, or not learning
    the way you think I should be learning, ask me about it.
    I might have an answer! I've been this way all my life,
    and I've come up with some ideas. Or we might come
    up with something together.

4. Just because I'm not doing something doesn't mean
    I'm being lazy. I may have more trouble figuring out
    what needs doing, especially in unstructured work. I may
    get overwhelmed when a lot of kids are doing different
    things at once. I might react by shutting down, or just
    sitting at my desk; or, being a kid, I might react by having
    a tantrum or being oppositional. If I am overwhelmed,
    I won't be able to work well (and what overwhelms me
    might not be what overwhelms other kids).

5. If I seem confused, I probably am. That doesn't mean
    I'm stupid or incapable, it just means I haven't understood
    something. What's clear to you may not be clear to
    me. Almost no one likes to appear confused or foolish,
    so it's very unlikely to be an act.

6. Specificity often helps. If you see me not performing properly, you might need to be more specific in what you want me to do.

7. I don't read body language well. Pretend I'm blind, if that helps. Or pretend you are writing to me rather than speaking. Would you give instructions differently? Then you'll be clearer to me, and I can learn.

8. Use labels in the classroom because I don't remember where things are. Expecting me to remember where everything is won't work, but labels usually will.

9. Everybody doesn't know what you think everybody knows. I (that's me personally, this time) don't know how to whistle, strike a match, make a bed, or fold a bag. But I can solve quadratic equations and do factor analysis. Let me do what I do well, and I will do it well.

10. If I ask for some kind of accommodation, I probably need it. The typical school accommodation, though, may not be right for me. For me (again me personally) extra time would have been no help at all—I was always done first!

Let me say I am all for teachers. Good teachers saved me. Teachers work harder than most people, at jobs that are more important than most jobs, for less money than a lot of jobs, and I thank them. The vast majority really care about kids. And, if you're a teacher who is reading this, you are one of that majority.

10: Standardized Testing and Interventions

Taking a standardized test is different from taking most other kinds of tests. Several techniques can help NLD students. The first thing is to realize that, on a standardized test, no one cares what you know or how you got an answer, they only care about the answer: Did you fill in the right circle?

So, the way to take a standardized test is to concentrate on the questions and answers, rather than the material. For example, on a reading comprehension test you may have to read a passage and then answer questions about it. Once the test is over, no one will care if you remember anything about the passage. This, then, requires a different sort of reading than most reading you do for school: You don't really have to understand what you are reading on any deep level, you don't need to store things in long-term memory; you just need to know the answers to the particular questions. So, you should read the questions before you read the passage. Then, you read the passage looking for the answers.

Suppose, for example, the passage is about the Civil War, and one of the questions is about the date some battle happened. Then, you can read the passage just looking for numbers and then find which number refers to the question. This should be very quick, and it can be very accurate. Or, if the question is about a person, then you can scan the passage just looking for capital letters (which might be a person's name) and only read more if it is about the person you are being asked about.

In mathematics questions, it can be even more important to look at the answers first. Sometimes, you can answer the question without doing any calculation at all. Other times, you can at least eliminate some of the choices.

Two critical skills on math tests of this type are estimation and digit checking, both of which I covered above.

There are several things you should know before you take any particular standardized test:

1. Is there a penalty for wrong answers, and if so, what is it?
2. Is the test given in traditional form, or as a computerized adaptive test?
3. Is the test given with pencil and paper, or on a computer, and how are answers marked?

Some tests penalize wrong answers, and some do not. Among those that do, the penalty can vary. Before taking the test, figure out what the best guessing strategy is. This depends on the number of choices and the guessing penalty. If, as is often the case, the test has five choices for each answer and each correct answer counts one point, then if there is a point penalty for guessing, then, on average, complete guessing will neither help nor hurt you. If, however, you can correctly eliminate one or more choices, then guessing will help you. If the penalty is less than a point, then even pure random guessing will help you. You need to investigate how the particular test you are interested in works.

In recent years, an increasing number of tests (including the Graduate Record Exam or GRE and the Graduate Management Admission Test or GMAT) have been given as computerized adaptive tests (CAT). In a standard test, everyone answers the same questions, and the more answers you get right, the higher your score. In a computerized adaptive test, everyone answers different questions, and your score depends on both which questions you answer and whether you get them right.

In a CAT, when you get a correct answer, the next question will be harder, and when you a wrong answer, the next question will be easier. In CATs, most people get about the same number of questions right, and test scores depend on which questions you are asked.

Although these seem very odd at first, they actually have several advantages over the traditional method.

In a traditional test, many of the questions are either much too hard or much too easy. Typically, each section starts with very easy questions, and ends with very hard ones. If a question is much too easy, you can only get it wrong by filling in the wrong circle, or some such mishap that has nothing to do with your ability. On the other hand, if a question is much too hard, you can only get it right by guessing, which also has nothing to do with ability.

In a CAT, however, most of the questions will be somewhat hard, and getting the right answer will depend mostly on your ability. This increases the amount of information that each question provides, and makes for more reliable tests.

The traditional standardized test is answered by filling in bubbles on a sheet that is separate from the question booklet. Such a procedure poses several problems for some NLDers:

1. Switching from the booklet to the scoring sheet
2. Filling the bubble in completely
3. Being sure to fill in the right bubble

If your NLD is severe, and you have a diagnosis, you may be able to get accommodations such as having more time, or having the test read to you, or being able to tell someone your answer choice.

In some newer tests, the test is given by computer and answers are through a keypad. You should find out ahead of time how this works on the test you have to take, and (if at all possible) practice under those conditions.

INTERVENTIONS

Many therapies are available, and many of them are helpful. But therapies can be a case where 1 + 1 may equal 2, but 1 + 1 + 1 does not equal 3 and, in fact, may be even less than 2. What I mean is that overscheduling an NLD child with therapies can be very unhelpful (Whitney, 2002).

Many children need down time and NLD children are likely to need more than most; in addition, NLD children may have a greater homework burden, in that it may take them more time than an NT child to do the work. Whitney (2002) and her family implement "slug nights" with her family where they would do no chores nor therapy; everyone would be lazy; instead of cooking, they ate takeout or leftovers. This can be an excellent way to have a calm day and can even act as family therapy.

PHYSICAL THERAPY (PT)

Physical therapy (PT) is more concerned with gross motor problems. PTs often deal with recovery from injury or surgery. They may have less relevance for NLDers.

OCCUPATIONAL THERAPY (OT)

Occupational therapy (OT) is usually concerned with fine motor problems. I know of many NLDers who have been helped by OT. In addition to things like handwriting, many OT know a lot about sensory problems. One technique that some have had success with is therapeutic listening. Others including balancing activities, help with use of scissors, copying shapes and working with materials like clay or silly putty. OTs can also work on mobility issues, from riding a scooter to driving a car

Occupational therapists can help children or adults with activities of daily living (ADL) such as dressing, basic cooking, and hygiene. They have training in teaching these skills and breaking them into small steps in ways that may not be apparent to parents. OTs may also help with a child's posture, gait, ability to sit (many NLD children fall out of their chairs) and other areas of physical functioning. This can even have application to children's physical safety (Whitney, 2002).

SPEECH AND LANGUAGE

Speech and language therapy can be about the act of making proper sounds; usually verbalizing is a strength of NLDers. Most often, NLDers need help with paralanguage–or interpreting and expressing body language in its many forms. They may also need help with the ability to deliver long statements, especially multi-step processes. For example, some NLDers will have trouble describing all the steps involved in a recipe. They may know how to make the recipe, but when asked to describe the steps, they may only be able to tell about the first few steps.

PSYCHOTHERAPY

Psychotherapy ("talk therapy") is somewhat controversial among NLD people. I found traditional therapy to be enormously useful, even life-saving. Others have found this sort of therapy ineffective. It is definitely an area where every individual is different. One question is whether the therapist has to know something about NLD before treating a person with NLD. Obviously, it is better if they do. The real question is whether it is *essential* that they do. My own experience is that it is not essential. When I was in therapy, almost no one, including my therapists and myself, had ever heard of NLD, yet therapy was helpful to me.

It is also important to remember that it is not so much a question of "is therapy good for people with NLD?" as it is "is *this* therapist good for *this* person with NLD?" A therapist who is wonderful with one person may not be good at all with another. For example, I once rejected a therapist after seeing him a couple times. He asked why. I said "Because I don't have any urge to call you by your first name." I wanted a therapist with whom I could be informal. Others might want just the reverse. This isn't a question of competence or ability, it's a question of matching of therapist with patient. I would also have a lot of trouble with a therapist who did not have a good sense of humor; despite the stereotype, I think this would be true for many NLDers.

These days, many more therapists have heard of NLD and other autism spectrum disorders, so, if you are considering this type of therapy for yourself or your child, it's probably worth looking for one who has at least heard of it. If you cannot find one, then you can list some of the issues you or your child is having that are NLD-related and see what the therapist knows about them and how he or she would treat them. With many NLD kids (and some NLD adults) a necessary precondition to this sort of therapy is unconditional positive regard (Whitney, 2002). This is not a method that all therapists endorse; failure to endorse it does not make a person a bad therapist, but it may well make him or her the wrong therapist for you or your child.

SOCIAL SKILLS GROUPS

Whitney (2002) notes that social skills groups can offer an opportunity for NLD kids to play with other children in a safe setting with a trained adult present. She states that there are four types of social skills groups, led by four different types of professionals: Psychology-based (led by either a psychiatrist, psychologist or social worker); speech based (led by a speech therapist); OT-based (led by an occupational therapist); and education-based (led by a teacher).

Each type of group has its own strengths and weaknesses. Which your child would benefit most from depends on his deficits and strengths.

VISION THERAPY

Vision therapy is about visual *perception* rather than visual *sensation* (which is the realm of an opthamologist or optometrist). An occupational therapist or a vision therapist gives vision therapy. It involves exercises that foster the ability to visualize.

For example, Whitney (2002) describes one exercise in which she drew a letter on her child's back and he had to then write it on a board. It can also involve recognizing shapes, colors, sorting items into categories based on visual characteristics. Since visualization happens continually throughout the day, there are many opportunities for intervention. For example, if your child is helping you cook, instead of saying, "Can you bring me a can of tomato sauce?" you could say, "Please bring me the sauce that's in a round, red can."

BEHAVIOR THERAPY

Behavior modification is generally not helpful for people with NLD unless it is addressing a behavior that the person can control (Whitney, 2002). If you think about it, this should really be obvious. No matter how much a behavior is rewarded or punished, if the person can't control whether he does it, it will not change. Often, behaviors that would be voluntary in NT people (or in those with some other conditions) are impossible in people with NLD. Therefore, behavior therapy, if used at all, must be used extremely cautiously. Rewarding behavior that is not under control is pointless; punishing behavior that is not in control is abusive.

TUTORING

If your NLDer is having academic problems and you have decided to hire a tutor, then I think it is very important that the person have as much understanding of both the subject matter and NLD as possible. NLDers often require different explanations than those that work for NT people. So, tutors have to understand the subject very well, so that they can offer alternative methods; and they have to know something about NLD, so that they know what alternatives to offer.

For example, if I wanted to hire a math tutor (for *any* grade level), I would investigate at local universities, not in the education department, but in the math department. I would try to find a graduate student who wanted to make some extra money, and who was interested in kids. Then I'd give him or her some materials on NLD, and we'd talk about the particular NLDer.

SPORTS

Many NLD people are physically maladroit. Personally, I was the last one picked on every team in school, and justifiably so: I can't run well, throw well, hit a baseball, kick well, and so on. Although some teams try to be more inclusive of people with lower levels of skill, it is nonetheless the case that, in a team sport, your teammates rely on you. If you play a team sport, others will see you playing it.

This can cause embarrassment, even with good will on all sides. In addition, most team sports emphasize precisely the skills that many NLD people are worst at: Hand-eye coordination; visual integration of a variety of stimuli (as when you have to figure out, quickly, where to throw a ball or where to run). I wouldn't say team sports can never be good for people with NLD, but it is not the first place I'd look.

Mamen (2007) points out another aspect of team sports that can cause problems for NLDers: Knowing where you are in space and where others are. This can be clearer when looking at someone at the opposite end of the skill level: Wayne Gretzky was a great hockey player largely because he knew, earlier than others, where the puck was going to be. Good players of any ball sport seem to know, very early, where the ball is headed, based either on strategy or physical cues or both.

Among the individual sports, swimming may be especially suited to NLD people. First, the role of hand-eye coordination is very limited; you need to be able to see the end of the pool, and that's about it. Second, it can help teach coordination between the two sides of the body, since both are used more or less identically.

Individual lessons may be very useful, especially at first. Be sure to tell the instructor of your child's (or your) needs: That verbal explanations are better than physical ones, for example. In group lessons, the students will be expected to follow a physical demonstration and the teacher will have less time to attend to each individual.

OTHER ACTIVITIES

MARTIAL ARTS

Martial arts, such as karate, can be very helpful for people with NLD. A good school and a good teacher will de-emphasize competition and will emphasize that the goal is to get better, however slowly that is done. However, some people with NLD will nevertheless compare themselves to others and may notice delays. Look for a dojo that does not emphasize which belt each student has at which age or time in training.

JUGGLING

Juggling is an interesting activity that helps many special needs children (or adults). It's got several advantages and is easier than most people realize. If you can toss a ball from hand to hand, you can learn to juggle. If you can toss a ball one handed, you can learn to juggle too.

- *It's noncompetitive.* Many sports and other physical activities are competitive. Certainly all team sports usually are, but many individual sports lend themselves to competition. Losing is part of competition. Unfortunately, it's a part that many special needs people are all too familiar with. If you can handle it, fine. But it's nice to do something where competition is not usually part of the deal. There are juggling competitions, but only a tiny percentage of jugglers take part in them.
- *You can practice anywhere.* If you are not very skilled at something, it can be embarrassing to do it in public. It's hard to swim or run without someone seeing you. But you can practice juggling anywhere.
- *It's something most people can't do at all.* Wouldn't it be nice, for once, to be able to do something that most "normal" people can't do?

Equipment for Juggling

Essentially, to learn the basic juggling moves, you need three objects, all the same size and shape. They should be small enough so you can hold two in one hand, but not much smaller than that, and heavy enough so you can easily feel them fall into your hand, but light enough so you can toss them easily. You'll be tossing them a lot. Beanbags work well, or, if you have some old tennis balls, you can cut a slit in each and insert about 10 pennies. This not only makes them a bit heavier, but will stop them from rolling too much when you drop.

Where to Practice
You can practice almost anywhere. One good spot is standing over a bed. Not only does this make it a lot easier to pick balls up when you drop, but it prevents you from moving forward to catch the balls; many people tend to throw the balls too far forward.

How to Juggle
The key in learning to juggle is to break it down into small steps and not go on to the next step too soon. The easiest juggle for most people is the three ball cascade (see below if you have use of only one hand).

Step 1—one ball. Take one ball (or beanbag, or whatever) in one hand. Toss it to the other hand. Then toss it back. Each toss should go to about eye height. Try not to look at the ball, except at the top of its arc. Practice until you barely have to move your hands to do this. Practice a lot. Some people get this quickly, some take a long time, but getting this step is the key, because this is what a three-ball cascade consists of.

Step 2—two balls, two tosses. Take two balls, one in each hand. Toss from your worst hand (for most people this is the left hand) then your better hand. The second toss should come when the first ball is at its peak. Then catch each. Then repeat. Repeat until this is easy. Toss toss catch catch.

Remember to watch the balls only at their peaks.

Step 3—two balls, many tosses. Start as before, but instead of left, right; left right; left right, do the following (assuming you are right handed). Toss from your left, then your right, then pause, then your right, then your left. That pause is where the third ball will go. Again, practice until this is easy.

Step 4—three balls. Start with two balls in one hand and one in the other. Toss from the hand with two balls and then do just as in step 3, but where the pause was, put another toss.

That's it! You're juggling!

Juggling with One Hand

Some people only have use of one hand. You can still learn to juggle. First step is to toss the ball over and over in the same hand. Then, add the second ball, and toss it when the first ball gets to the peak of its arc.

This is harder than the three ball cascade, but it can be done.

Where to Go from Here?

This could be all the juggling you ever learn, and that's fine. But if you want to learn more, a good place to look is the International Jugglers Association.

Happy juggling!

11: Adulthood— Ready or Not!

WHAT HAPPENS TO KIDS WITH NLD? THEY TURN INTO ADULTS with NLD! While there is little material about NLD kids, there is virtually none about NLD adults. What's life like for adults with NLD? Let's look at work, relationships, and everything else.

THE WORK WORLD

There are three big switches in most people's lives: home to school, school to work, work to retirement. In your first years, you're at home with your parents or caregivers. Then you spend a long time in school with teachers and classmates. Then you leave school and begin work with colleagues and bosses. Then you retire.

This section considers the second of these big switches: School to work

In the United States, you are owed an education. The school system may not deliver what it owes—all too often it does a miserable job of delivering. But in theory, you have the right to a free and appropriate education. You may need a lot of persistence and advocates to get it, but you are owed it.

All this changes when you go to work.

Your boss does not owe you a job.

It is true that there are laws against workplace discrimination, but that is quite different. Companies exist to make money, not to employ people. You are, therefore, employed to help a company make money. Once you really realize this, your perspective should change.

The work world is very different from the school world, and many (perhaps most) NLDers find the work world much more challenging. The saying about square pegs and round holes is an apt description. However, a square peg will fit in a round hole if the hole is big enough. The art of success at work involves both the peg (the NLD person) and the hole (the job). It also requires a new attitude on the part of the NLDer.

Rather than demanding accommodations (as you could in school) you should make accommodations. And you should sell those accommodations to your employers by showing them how the accommodations help them, not how they help you. For example, I know some people use special keyboards to type on.

If you go to your boss and demand that he (or she) buy one for you then she (or he) may well tell you to forget it. Or fill out some form in triplicate. Or they may just mark you in their heads as being a pain in the *** and start looking for reasons to fire you.

And once someone starts thinking about you in a negative way, this negativity expands to other areas too. This happens automatically (it's called the halo effect), and it happens to just about everyone. That is, once you are seen as a problem case, then everything you do—good or bad—is viewed from that perspective.

On the other hand, if you bring a keyboard in and just start using it, you risk violating some rule or other. Not as bad as the first alternative, but still not good.

But what if you go to your boss when he (or she) has a minute and say, "You know, my job requires a lot of typing. I'd like to type as quickly and accurately as possible, so that I can get more work done and help you as much as I can. That's easier for me if I use this special keyboard. I brought one in. Could I use it?"

No more pain in the *** and now your boss may be motivated to help you get around any rules.

That's just one example. It works with any accommodation you might need.

Self-advocate. Unfortunately, the accommodations at work are not mandated and not standard.

You have to self-advocate. The process of getting an accommodation at work is a two stages.

>
> ***First, figure out what accommodation you need.*** First, you figure out what your issue is. In other words, what are you accommodating? A common issue for NLDers is preferring things in writing to things in speech. This may arise from the fact that much of speech is nonverbal and we often don't get that part. Also, many of us NLDers are highly literate or have good reading comprehension. So, the need is a problem with verbal communication.
>
> Next, think through how your need could be accommodated. Brainstorm! Ask on NLD-in-common or NLD-Adult. (See Resources, page 159.) Think about how this was dealt with in school. Make a list. Then narrow it down. Ask yourself, what would work in the workplace? Perhaps you taped lectures and then took notes later. That could be easy: Just ask your boss. Figure out what could work for you and your boss.
>
> ***Second, you have to get the accommodation.*** In school you were owed accommodations (unless you're middle aged or older, like me—we got zip). At work, this is rarely the case. So you have to self-advocate. The key to self-advocacy is to make it be in the other person's interest to help.

Use your smarts. Rather than making demands, make yourself useful to an employer. This is an art and requires ingenuity. But being good at it yields rewards. Some examples may clarify what I mean.

A former physician of mine grew up during the Great Depression. He applied for a summer job, standing on a long line of applicants for a single job. In those days, many places had ice-boxes instead of refrigerators. A large block of ice was melting in the sun near the line of applicants. He walked over, picked it up, brought it inside, and asked someone where he should put it. They sent all the other boys home, and gave him the job.

My brother once had a summer job hanging posters in record stores. Lots of other kids had had similar jobs in previous summers, and none of them had been offered full-time position. My brother, though, would notice things and report back on his ideas. For instance, he would notice if his company's records were prominently displayed and figure out ways to make them more prominent. He got a job that fall.

Time to talk. I heard of a man whose job required sitting in meetings. He, like many with NLDers (including me), had trouble with talking too much. To solve this problem, he did two things: First, he learned a couple rules, like "Always let your boss talk first," and, second, he asked a helpful coworker to sit next to him and signal him by touching his elbow when he was talking too much.

If you have a good friend at work, or someone who works in a similar job as yours, you can consult with them about proper and improper workplace behavior. You also might ask about this sort of thing is on one of the mailing lists about NLD. See Resources, page 159.

The keys to success on a job are:

- Find out what you can do to help an employer, and which employer needs it.
- Find out what you can't do well, and ways you can get around that mountain or avoid that mountain. See Chapter 5 for more on the mountain strategy.

Know yourself. Another help is knowing yourself. If you are just starting out, I strongly recommend learning all you can about yourself as a potential employee, which is, as I said, a very different role from being a student. There are many ways to learn yourself, but none that I know of are geared specifically to NLD people. One way to learn about yourself is to try to list your strengths and weaknesses. You might divide them up into categories such as:

- Cognitive
- Physical
- Emotional
- Social

Don't try to limit your list to things you think of as job-related. There are all sorts of jobs, and your strengths and weaknesses will affect how you perform each of them. Many people fail to recognize both these facts people aren't aware of how many jobs there are, because they tend to know people who do similar jobs to their own. And most people, especially NT people, tend to underestimate how much a person's strengths and weaknesses affect performance, because most people don't have the extremes of strengths and weaknesses that NLDers have.

Once you have a long list, start thinking about careers. Many public libraries have a good information on different jobs, although it may not be clear which jobs demand which skills.

Below, I've listed some jobs that NLDers do well, based on information from the Yahoo newsgroups and books listed in Resources, especially Fast's book.

Great jobs for NLDers. If you find a job that you think you might want to pursue, you should try to ask as many people as you can about the job. Once you've found a person who has the job you are interested in, talk to him or her about it. Most people like to talk about themselves and their work. Ask what they do in a typical day, and if they spend much time doing things you are bad at. Another thing to do is try to find biographies or autobiographies written by people who are prominent in that field.

Jobs that NLD people have had success include:

- **Accountant.** Accountants focus on figures. Although numeric thinking is important, higher math is not needed. Attention to detail is important.
- **Animal trainer or veterinary work.** Many NLDers love animals. Human interaction is minimized.
- **Archival or library science** which may include cataloguing work where attention to detail is important and social skills minimal.
- **College professor** which can involve highly specialized knowledge. As noted, academic settings tend to be tolerant of eccentric people and unusual behavior.
- **Lawyer** especially legal research. The legal profession has a vast array of jobs. Although the most well-known specialty is the trial lawyer (which is ill-suited for most NLDers), most attorneys never venture into a courtroom. In addition, a job like a paralegal requires less education and executive functioning.
- **Statistician** which is my profession. Although many NLD people have trouble with math, some excel in math. Many

statisticians work alone or have limited interpersonal contact. "Nerdy-ness" is expected.

- **Writer** especially of nonfiction. Nonfiction writers usually do a lot of research, a strength of NLDers. Writers often work alone so they create their own methods of doing things and choose their own schedules. Some nonfiction writing is formulaic, where the writer fills in details—an example is training manuals—eliminating some tasks that are weaknesses for some NLD people.
- **Researcher.** Many people need to get research done by someone else. I talked a little about legal research, but research and fact checking are also needed by journalists, academics, politicians, and many not-for-profit groups.
- **Editor**—Many NLDers love facts and are good at remembering them; many are also good with words. Also, many like the act of correcting. This makes the various jobs within editing and proofreading appealing (Whitney 2002).

Not-so-great jobs for NLDers. There are also many types of jobs where NLD people may not do well. In particular, many of us do badly at jobs that require the following:

- Physical coordination (e.g., waiter/waitress)
- Immediate personal connections with people (e.g., sales person)
- Multitasking, or rapid switching of tasks (e.g., managerial positions)
- Strong nonverbal skill (e.g., actor, sales person, politician)

Of course, there are exceptions to all these rules; you have to base your job choice on self-knowledge. Nevertheless, I think it likely that NLDers are more likely to find success if they look in fields that do not require these skills.

Preferences. It's important to find a job that you suits your workplace preferences. If everyone dresses formally and you hate wearing a suit or dress, then that may not be the place for you. That's relatively easy to tell on an interview. Other aspects of workplace culture may be harder to assess, but remember that the interview is not just a chance for them to see it they want to hire you, it's also a chance for you to see if you want to work there. For example, if the interview involves a lot of hassling-type questions, this may be a sign that it is a highly stressful workplace. If you don't thrive on that, then it may not be right for you.

A way to learn which type of workplaces fit you is to get some professional career counseling. It typically involves testing, much of which may be informative. One test is the Strong Campbell Interest Inventory. This consists in answering many questions about what you would prefer to do (e.g., "would you rather take a walk in the country or go to a concert?"). Your answers are then compared to the answers of people who are successful in various jobs. People tend to like jobs where there are a lot of people with similar answers.

Some work environments are more tolerant of quirky behavior than others. In my experience, academic and research environments are much more tolerant that business environments. Not-for-profit organizations tend to be more accepting, as well. Exceptions to this guideline are the "back-office" jobs at some businesses, including investment. If you are good at picking stocks, then a lot will be forgiven. I worked one summer at a Wall Street company, and saw many people who had major social problems, but these problems were tolerated because the people were good at their jobs, and because the job did not involve direct customer contact.

Disclosure. In the workplace, should you tell your prospective employer or your coworkers that you have NLD?

When considering disclosure, think through these questions:

- Who should you tell?
- When should you tell?
- What should you tell?
- How should you tell?

Unfortunately, none of these questions has definitive answers that work for every person and every job. All of the answers will depend on the type of job. Is a single person hiring you? A small company? A large corporation? Is the job short-term or long-term? Is it entry level, or is it one where you have already evidenced a set of skills from past work?

Here's some advice and suggestions.

Who and when should you tell? You might tell the personnel or human resources department during the hiring process, you might tell your boss either during the interview or right after you get hired, or later on; you might tell your colleagues either soon after you get hired or later on.

There are advantages and disadvantages to each. If you disclose early in the hiring process, then you can never be accused of trying to hide something, but you may hurt your chances of getting the job or be accused of seeking special treatment. I think the first part of this is not really that much of an issue. If a company refuses to hire people with disabilities, not only are they breaking the law, but they are probably not a company you want to work for, anyway. The problem of seeming to seek special treatment can be ameliorated by telling in the right way (see below). So, I generally favor telling people about NLD relatively early in the process.

The question of telling your colleagues is more personal. I think it is usually best to wait a while until you've made a friend or two. It can be very helpful to have a colleague who knows about your problems and who can provide valuable advice about coping with different people and different situations.

What and how should you tell? I have some fairly strong opinions about what and how to tell. I don't think it's a good idea to just say, "I have NLD." It may not even be a good idea to use the NLD phrase at all. It's not well known, and even less well understood. But if you use it, people may feel awkward asking you about it either because they don't want to feel ignorant or because they don't want to embarrass you, or possibly for fear of a lawsuit by asking too many questions.

Instead, describe what your difficulties are, how you think they might affect the job, and what you plan to do to ameliorate these problem. This gets right into how you should tell. If you tell your boss or the personnel department, you should not go in trying to get your boss or your company to do things for you. Rather, you should go in trying to do something for them. Even after getting a job, you still have to sell yourself. Make it clear that you want to help them do their job better, make more money, serve more clients, or whatever, and you will have them on your side.

TEN THINGS WE WISH OUR BOSSES KNEW

Right now, I work for myself. I'm a statistical consultant as well as a consultant on learning disabilities. But I've had bosses, and so have other people with NLD. This is a sort of pastiche.

1. Just because I'm disabled doesn't mean I'm not abled. There are things I can do badly, there are things I can do well and there are some things I can't do at all. The fact that some of the things I can't do at all are easy for you, doesn't mean that some of things I can do well aren't hard

for you. If you let me do what I'm good at, I can do my job better, and that helps you do better too.

2. I often need instructions in a different way; that doesn't mean I can't learn. Some of us learn better by listening, some by reading, and some by watching someone do a task. Don't assume that I am not interested in learning just because your instructions didn't seem to take; I might need them in a different format. Once I've figured out the instructions, I can do my job better, and that helps you do better too.

3. You can ask me questions. If you notice that I'm not doing what you think I should be doing, or not learning the way you think I should be learning, ask me about it. I might have an answer! I've been this way all my life, and I've come up with some ideas. Or we might come up with something together. Then I can do my job better, which will help you do better too.

4. Just because I'm not doing something doesn't mean I'm being lazy. I may have more trouble figuring out what needs doing, especially in unstructured work. I may get overwhelmed when a lot of people are doing different things at once. I might react by shutting down, or just sitting at my desk. But if you ask me to do something, I will try to do it. Or if there is a list of tasks to be done, with their priorities listed, I can look at that. But if I am overwhelmed, I won't be able to do my job, and that makes your job harder too.

5. If I seem confused, I probably am. That doesn't mean I'm stupid or incapable, it just means I haven't understood something. What's clear to you may not be clear to me. If we are both clear on what you've said, then we can both do our jobs better.

6. Specificity often helps. If you see me not performing properly, you might need to be more specific in what you want me to do. Then I can do my job better, and you'll look better too.

7. I don't read body language well. Pretend I'm blind, if that helps. Or pretend you are writing to me rather than speaking. Would you give instructions differently? Then you'll be clearer to me, and we can both do our jobs better.

8. On the other hand, labels on things do help. Because I don't remember where things are. Expecting me to remember where everything is won't work, but labels usually will. Then you can spend less time telling me where things are, and more time doing your job.

9. Everybody doesn't know what you think everybody knows. I (that's me personally, this time) don't know how to whistle, strike a match, make a bed or fold a bag. But I can solve quadratic equations and do factor analysis. Let me do what I do well, and I will do it well. And then you can do what you do well, too.

10. If I ask for some kind of accommodation, I probably need it. If you can't make that particular accommodation, then let's discuss it so we can both do our jobs better.

ROMANTIC RELATIONSHIPS

Although NLD poses numerous problems, people with NLD can have fulfilling romantic relationships, including marriage.

Meeting someone. This is the first step for getting into a relationship. Many women with NLD report being unaware that men are flirting with them. They learn about the flirting after female friends tell them. Much, probably an overwhelming amount, of flirting is done nonverbally, in exactly the ways that NLDers have trouble comprehending.

NLDers can also be very bad at the active side of flirtation. Since we much prefer language to other methods of communication, we can come across as overbearing or aggressive, simply because the NT world prefers nonverbal communication to indicate romantic interest in someone.

I think that computers, and especially the Internet, can be a great boon to NLDers in this aspect of their lives. One can meet people on the Internet, not necessarily (maybe not even advisedly) in the sites devoted to dating. There are e-mailing lists, blogs, and chat rooms devoted to a huge range of topics. On the Internet, NTers are forced to communicate with us in the ways that we like; you can't type body language or eye contact into a computer. Once you have become friends with someone online, it is much easier for them to accept you in person. I have even heard of couples who got engaged to be married before they ever met, face to face.

Keeping a relationship. Of course, finding someone to be in a relationship with is only the beginning. You then have to figure out how to maintain the relationship. The huge number of books and other materials on dating is geared toward the general (that is, NT) audience, and they suggest that maintaining a relationship is not easy, even for people without NLD. It is more difficult for NLDers. As far as I know, no specific research has been done on romantic relationships with NLDers. Some has been done on conditions like Asperger's, but I think NLD is sufficiently different that new research is needed.

The relational difficulties for NLDers mainly arise, I think, because it is so hard to explain our difficulties in ways that the other person can understand and adapt to. In some ways, men with NLD are like the prototypical male in relationships; we want to be told things explicitly and directly, and we to communicate explicitly and directly. An issue women with NLD face is they aren't big on chitchat, romantic or otherwise. For NLDers in general, communication in intimate relationships is a challenge because it is dependent on knowing the other's particular looks, moods, expressions and so on.

Getting married. Despite the difficulties of meeting someone and dating, some NLDers are married. I've been married for over 20 years, and I know of several other couples where one person is NLD. Marriage for NLDers is possible. But it isn't easy.

As researchers learn more about how NLD affects relationships, some difficulties can be ameliorated.

EVERYTHING ELSE

Speaking from experience, from work to relations to everything else, every day is a new adventure! OK, maybe not *every* day. But our lives are filled with adventures that NT people can only try to imagine.

Here are some adventures of mine.

PARKING LOTS

Parking lots are horrible places. Not, probably, for you neurotypical people. From what I can tell, you park your cars, note where they are, and, later, find them.

For me and others with NLD, it's different. Personally, I don't drive so I don't park my car. But I ride in cars and sometimes separate from the other passengers at a destination. I *try* to remember something about where the car is: a numbered spot, for example. But often I wander, aimlessly, looking for the car. Of course, I've likely forgotten the make and color of the car, which doesn't help either.

Often I end up calling another passenger and telling that person where I am. Then they come get me and take me to the car.

WHAT COLOR IS MY ROOM?

The other day I was trying to describe to my therapist how my disability works. Those of you who have tried to do describe NLD know this isn't easy. Describing some LDs is easier: Dyslexia involves trouble with reading; dyscalculia involves trouble with math. There are subtleties, but the general notion is clear. What exactly does NLD cause trouble with? Sometimes I say "space and time."

One of my problems is very little visual memory. Most people don't seem to really get it when I say that. Oh, they know the words…but don't get it. I told my therapist that I don't remember the color of my bedroom walls. This struck her as remarkable. It turns out that she could easily remember the color of all the rooms in her apartment. She thought this was pretty usual even though she doubted she has an unusually good visual memory.

So, when I returned home after my session, I looked at my bedroom walls. They are yellow. The ceiling is white. I now remember that. But I remember it verbally "walls are yellow, ceiling is white" rather than visually.

MAKING THE BED

A lot of people make their bed every morning. Maybe you're one of them. And, if you're NT, it's probably pretty simple. You probably do it the same way, each time. There's some set of steps you follow, and, in the end, you have a made bed. Maybe it doesn't have hospital corners, but it's made.

Well, it's different for some of us NLDers. I usually don't make the bed. (OK, I'm a slob). But when I do try, there's no set of steps to follow. There's a couple sheets, a blanket, and a bed. And so, I try to figure out what to do. The fitted sheet goes on first, I know that. But which way? Does one side go up and one down (toward the mattress?) Which is width and which is length?

I don't know. I never know. I try random things and eventually one works. Then the top sheet. Same problem. The blanket is easier, because it's reversible in both directions.

It can take me a long time and a lot of frustration to make the bed. It doesn't seem to get easier over time. So, I don't do it.

(But if you have any quadratic equations you need solved, I'm your guy).

WHERE DOES THE SUN RISE?

Way back when I was age 10 or so, I took a bunch of psychological tests. One of them was an IQ test—the WISC. These scales certainly have their issues, but they can provide useful information when used properly by experts. One such piece of information is the pattern of subtest scores. One subtest on the WISC is called "information" and it's more or less what it sounds like: general information questions. My fund of general information (then and now) is pretty good. But one question stumped me, early in the test, a question most 10-year-old kids probably could answer: **Where does the sun rise?**

I didn't know, but I tried to figure it out.

The "easy" way to figure this out would be to think about my walk to school: Due east into the rising sun. But that didn't work for me. I couldn't remember if I saw the sun rising on my way to school. I tried to remember where the sun was that day, but I took the test in midwinter, and the sun in winter rises in the south, more or less. No good. I knew he wanted east or west. So, I tried reasoning about the spin of the Earth, and time zones; I knew it was earlier in the west, so that had to mean something, but I didn't figure it out in time. I guessed and I guessed wrong. Luckily for my score on that subtest, I got all the other questions right.

So, now, I remember where the sun rises. How do I do this? Easy. The word *sets* is almost a rhyme and almost an anagram of *west*. So, I just remember "sets in the wets" and then convert it to west. *Voila!*

LOST

A couple weeks ago I went to a friend's house for dinner. I've been there many times before–dozens of times, I think. I got lost. Again.

I live in Manhattan, and most of Manhattan is a grid, which is great for me. Not only is it a grid, but the streets are numbered. I can remember 78, 79, 80. I know how that works. Some avenues are numbered, some aren't. But there aren't that many of them, so I can more or less get by. And I know some tricks (for instance, on the streets, which run east to west, the odd numbered buildings are on the north side of the street. So, if I come out of an odd numbered building on a street, I know I am facing south. Sadly there is no such rule for avenues. In most of Manhattan, I manage.

But the friend I mentioned lives in Greenwich Village, and it's not a grid at all. So I took the subway to the right stop. Then I started walking in the right direction. Then I turned at the wrong spot and wandered in a sort of spiral, eventually getting to his building.

I don't know how people find places where the whole city is full of streets that aren't numbered or organized in ways that aren't grids.

DO WE HAVE A TOASTER OVEN?

Before reading on, answer me this: Do you have a toaster oven? If so, where is it? And did you have to go search for it?

One day, I was reading a cookbook and I decided to make a toasted sandwich. The book said to cook it in a toaster oven. Hmm. Do we have a toaster oven? I don't know, but I know who to ask! My wife.

"Hey Les, do we have a toaster oven?"

"It's on the counter, next to the coffee maker you use every morning."

I look and **there it is**! How could I not know that the toaster oven is there? I saw it every day! Most days, I saw it several times. But I don't remember things that way.

TICK TOCK

I have troubles with time. I have no problem *telling* time. As far as I know, I learned to read a clock at a normal age. But I have trouble knowing when things happened and with knowing how long things take. Since I don't know how long things take, I have trouble answering the question:

When should I leave?

The other day I needed to pick up my son at camp. The camp is about 1 1/2 miles from my home and it's right on a subway line, which I've taken many times. And I've been to the camp before, too. I had to be there at 2 p.m. So when should I leave my apartment to pick up my son? I don't know. I arrived 20 minutes early, after a 15-minute trip.

In about 10 days, we're going to the airport. I know the time of departure, and I've been to that airport many times. But…

When should I leave?

I don't know. This time, I can ask my wife. She knows. Even better, we'll probably order a car service to take the four of us and our luggage to the airport. The car service will know, too.

I have to get to work by a certain time. *When should I leave?*
I have to get home by a certain time. *When should I leave?*

Unless it is something I have done many times, I don't know. So, I always overestimate the time it will take. And I always bring a book.

12: Hope, Help, and Happiness

ALL PEOPLE, WHATEVER THEIR ABILITIES OR DISABILITIES, DE-serve to be treated with dignity. Dignity is **the quality or state of being worthy of esteem or respect. People treated with dignity have hope.**

What does dignity mean when dealing with people who are learning disabled and, more specifically, who have NLD? To me, it means recognizing the importance of all three words in the phrase "learning disabled person." There are, then, two ways to fail to esteem and respect a person who is learning disabled: You can fail to recognize that we are people or you can fail to recognize that we are disabled. Often, people are so intent on avoiding the first error that they commit the second one.

I read a teacher's blog post and said she the term learning disability is baloney. She made an analogy to blindness. She said that blind people could not see, but people with LD can learn. I certainly agree that LD people can learn and blind people can't see. But blindness is not the only disability, even with regard to vision, and the disability of blindness is not just not being able to see, but not being able to get around the inability. Just as there are tools to help the blind (e.g., canes, seeing-eye dogs, braille, and so on), there are tools to help people with LD. Further, extreme nearsightedness is also a disability, even though such people can see.

When you deny that LD people have a disability, you disrespect us; you fail to treat us with dignity. There are things that most people can do with little difficulty that LD people can do only with difficulty or not at all. A blind person can learn to walk and avoid tripping or crashing, but cannot learn to drive in traffic.

One of the tricky parts of NLD is figuring out just what the person can do, cannot do at all, or can do only with difficulty. The person is, himself a good but not infallible guide to this. Yet you must also not make the other error. LD people are people. Treating us or referring to them as if they were not is also failing to respect us. This can be a difficult line to walk! But we didn't make it hard for you on purpose.

HOW TO WASTE TIME AND IRRITATE PEOPLE (ESPECIALLY NLDERS)

Do you like wasting your time? Probably not.

Do you like irritating people? I hope not! (Although, looking at how some people behave...)

Why not read the following list on "how to waste time and irritate people" and determine to do the opposite?

So how can you waste your time and irritate people, especially us NLDers?

- Communicate in ways we can't understand. If you knew someone didn't speak English at all, would you speak English to them? I hope not. If you knew someone spoke very little English, would you speak as you normally do? Or might you use simpler words and speak more slowly? (Some people speak more loudly to NLDers, which strikes me as odd. I hear just fine.) Yet many people assume that we NLDers will "get" their body language and tone of voice, even after we tell them that we don't.

- Ask us questions we can't answer. I never know where anything is. A lot of NLDers have similar problems. So, please don't ask us where things are. There are lots of other questions I cannot answer. What did he look like? How do I get there? How old was I when something happened? How long will it take to get there? What should I wear? I DON'T KNOW!
- Get mad at us NLDers for things we can't help. It can be irritating dealing with people who have a disability. We are, in some ways, harder to deal with that people without disabilities. But we didn't choose our disability. So, instead of getting mad at us for things we cannot help, express your irritation some other way. Even better, try to work out ways to get around your irritation. Because just like you don't like being irritated, we don't like irritating you.

Yes, I'm disabled. More specifically, I'm learning disabled. Even more specifically, I have nonverbal learning disabilities. Not differences, disabilities. There are things that virtually all NT people. A "difference" is something you might choose—more rational or more emotional? More mathematical or more artistic? A disability is something you wouldn't choose, and I'm disabled. I am, that is, UNable to do some things. Hence the word.

But I am also abled. Here's a little line under "abled" to remind me that world thinks it isn't a word. Isn't that a commentary on the world? That is, we have no problem (and no red line) with **disabled** but we have a hard time with **abled.** Why should that be?

Not only am I abled, in some ways I am more able than the average NT. I am better at math than the average NT person; I also read and spell well. And my grammar doesn't stink. (I'm also insanely modest, but don't tell anyone).

When people hear the word "disabled," I think they may picture a cripple. (I use this offensive term deliberately.) They think of a beggar on the street or a person living in a sheltered environment, unable to care for themselves. Some of us are like that; and, of course, some of you NT people are like that too.

Or else they leap to an image of Helen Keller (blind, deaf, summa cum laude graduate of Radcliffe) and, yes, some of us are like that, too. As are some of you NT people.

Most of us, though, are like you. Abled. Not supremely gifted. Not geniuses. Most of us don't win Nobel prizes, go to the Olympics, or write best-selling novels. And, in fact, most of you don't, either. Those are extraordinary accomplishments, and they are called extraordinary because they are outside (extra) the ordinary. Most of us are ordinary. We just have some more severe deficits than you do.

In graduate school, I had a hard time figuring out how to get from the bus stop to class. After getting my Ph.D., I still got lost on the way home from work. Even though I can do statistics, I can't figure out how to fold a paper bag or make a bed or strike a match; I still can't visualize anything, and I still mis-estimate the time it will take to do things. I'm disabled. But I'm also abled.

Most of us disabled people are like that. Doing our best, trying to cope.

MOVING FORWARD

There are more reasons for hope, there is some help available, and happiness is possible. I am not a Pollyanna, but neither will I deny that it is possible to have a good, fulfilling, and happy life with NLD. Not, perhaps, an *easy* life, but then, few people really do have easy lives. Nor, by and large, do easy things offer much fulfillment. If you watch children who have just learned some new skill, you will see their faces light up. Once that skill is mastered, it ceases to give such joy. You and I do not thrill ourselves when we push an elevator button, or remember that 5 and 5 make 10.

HOPE

Admitting or discovering that your child or that you have NLD can be quite painful. Some of the literature (particularly the earlier literature, including the work of Byron Rourke) is very gloomy. As I said, I am not a Pollyanna, and I am not going to pretend that life with NLD is easy. I call it a disability because it disables me. But NLD is only part of who I am, and it is only part of who your child is. Having NLD is a handicap, but it is not the clap of doom. Many people with NLD have good jobs, fulfilling relationships, and satisfying lives. They've learned to cope, and they are reason for you to have hope; not hope that your child will be exactly like them: he is not them. Hope, rather, that people with problems similar to those your child has have succeeded, and that this indicates that he, with his different but similar problems, can also succeed. You shouldn't try to deny your child's disability, but neither should you wallow in it.

HELP

If you are the parent of a child, then there is even more reason for hope, because help is available now that was simply not available years ago. I covered a lot of interventions in Chapter 10.

People have learned a lot about NLD and other similar problems, and they are still learning more. Although NLD is still not as widely known as dyslexia or ADHD, it is becoming familiar to more and more people. Later in this book I offer some suggestions on getting help in specific areas. Here, I will give some general guidelines.

I should stress that if you are feeling suicidal, or if you suspect a child you care about is feeling suicidal, you should seek professional help *immediately*. There are a number of suicide helplines, one is 1-800-273-8255. You may wish to share some of the strategies I talk about here with a therapist, but they are not a substitute for therapy. Suicide is *not* a good solution to the problems of NLD or any other LD, and this book is *not* sufficient for dealing with these issues. I'm not a therapist, and even if I was, no book is sufficient for these issues.

HAPPINESS

I've rephrased the famous saying "anything worth doing is worth doing well." Years ago, as a counter to the cult of mastery, I started using the phrase "anything worth doing is worth doing badly." Then I found out that G. K. Chesterton originated the famous saying. It's certainly true that some things *must* be done well: A surgeon has to know what he or she is doing. And, to earn a living, you have to know how to do at least one thing well.

But many things that are worth doing are worth doing badly—singing, for example. Now, if you sing poorly you shouldn't make others *listen* to your singing. But if it gives you pleasure to sing, then sing! I like to play bridge; I am not very good and likely never will be. But I like it. So?

So I will never be a world champion or even club champion. So what?

The original saying is, I suppose, intended to inspire greater effort and attention to detail. But I think it enforces an entirely wrong standard. It emphasizes mastery instead of enjoyment. Very few humans, NLDers or not, are exceptional at many things. We do need to be good at *some* things, of course. An example is driving. Society should keep incompetent drivers off the road; this is why we require people to get licenses to drive.

There is much more to life than making a living and activities like driving. Yet the cult of mastery seems to say that the only worthwhile activities are those we master. Why? Why deny people the pleasure they get from doing things, even things they are bad at?

My advice is this: If you like to sing, sing. If you sing badly, then you may not want to sing in public. But if your singing annoys no one and gives you pleasure, do it.

Not only does this attitude allow people (especially those with disabilities) to take pleasure in more activities, but it fosters a lack of embarrassment at one's one own failures. Indeed, if one's sole goal from an activity is enjoyment, then failure is redefined. It is true that there are many things we NLDers will not be good at. But it is also true that there are many things that individual NTers will not be good at, either. In addition, while we NLDers may not improve as rapidly with practice as NT people do, we will improve. It's much easier to practice things that you enjoy. Thus, by de-emphasizing mastery we may actually increase it.

For example, suppose one likes to swim. One way (the traditional way, which I think is overemphasized) is to judge success at swimming by how fast or how long you can swim, by whether you can compete in races, and so on. The other way is to ask yourself if you enjoy swimming. You may never win a race, or even compete in a race. But if you enjoy the activity, then you are winning when you do it, even if your strokes aren't right, you aren't fast, and you can't swim very long. Yet, if you keep swimming, you may want to swim better, and this may increase your enjoyment. Certainly anyone who swims can learn to swim better, even if the end-goal of that improvement is not winning a race, or even swimming faster, but simply enjoying oneself more.

Closing Thoughts On Disablity

Yes, disability implies something is wrong. And, at least for me, something *is* wrong. To deny it (as many people did during my childhood, and still do somewhat today) is kind of insulting in a weird way; it says that my difficulties are my fault. Each person is different from everyone else. *Some* of us are disabled.

I am also very nearsighted and see out of only one eye. This is also a disability, and people accept it and might say, "Oh, he's nearsighted." This is not an insult, it's a statement of fact. My eyeglasses mostly correct my nearsightedness. Doctors cannot improve my loss of vision in one eye. (I had an operation at age 3 that didn't work; I've tried vision therapy to no avail). With one good eye, my depth perception stinks. And if I explain this to people, neither they nor I have any problem saying that this is something wrong with me.

I suppose I could call myself "differently-sighted" but that's silly.

There's no stigma to vision problems.

When it comes to learning disabilities, stigma exists.

There are other things I cannot accomplish that most people do easily.

For instance, I cannot draw. *At all.* Drawing a simple shape like a cylinder is impossible for me. My wife is an artist, and she has tried to teach me. I have an MA in special education, and art therapists have tried to teach me. My brain doesn't *do* that.

Other examples: I get lost. *All the time.* I can't estimate time. I can't remember when things happened. These are disabilities too. It is *better* to have the ability to find your way to a friend's house than to get lost. Leaving the subway and going straight to my destination is *better* than wandering around lost. (Just yesterday, on my way to give a presentation on recursive partitioning, I wandered around lost, and I had been to the place several times.)

These example describe disabilities whether you call them NLD, AS, learning problems, learning disabilities, learning differences, or kumquats.

But there's that stigma.

How do we get rid of the stigma? By claiming it, not by denying it.

So, when someone says something like, "You can't be learning disabled, you have a Ph.D.," I say "Yes, I can. It's just that I'm good at academic subjects." If a longer conversation ensues, I may point out the many things that most people learn to do — like finding your way home.

There are some things wrong with me; there are some things right with me.

The things that are wrong don't make me evil, bad, lazy, crazy, or stupid; they make me disabled.

The things that are right with me don't make me good, energetic, sane, or smart; they make me gifted.

Together, along with a lot of other stuff, they make me Peter.

Resources

Recommended Books

Bridging the Gap: Raising a Child with Nonverbal Learning Disorder. Rondalyn Varney Whitney is both the mom of an NLD child and a pediatric occupational therapist specializing in NLD. There is also an extensive though slightly dated list of references.

Employment for People with Nonverbal Learning Disabilities and Asperger's Syndrome: Stories and Strategies. Yvona Fasts' book is excellent for people who want to know how to find a job, what sorts of jobs work for NLDers (and what sorts do not), and ways to improve the chance of success on the job.

Helping the Child Who Doesn't Fit In. This helpful book by S. Norwicki and M.P. Duke is geared more generally, to both parents and professionals.

It's So Much Work to Be Your Friend. Richard Lavoie, more than a lot of authors, understands what it feels like to be learning disabled LD and is able to communicate that feeling to others. Although the book covers all sorts of LD, it is relevant to NLD.

The Out of Sync Child. New York: Penguin, 2006. This book by Carol Kranowitz focuses on sensory integration disorder, which is not uncommon among NLDers.

Teaching Your Child the Language of Social Success. As the title indicates, this book by M.P. Duke et al is for parents of NLD children. It contains useful exercises to improve some the social skills of NLD kids. With a little creativity, many of these could be adapted for older children and adults.

The Source for Nonverbal Learning Disabilities by Sue Thompson.

A Special Kind of Brain: Living with Nonverbal Learning Disability. A biography that shares the story of how Nancy Burger learned how to help her son.

Syndrome of Nonverbal Learning Disorder. Byron Rourke is the one who first provided the diagnosis of NLD. Keep this in mind while reading his book: He wrote about the NLD people he knew—the most severely affected adults, none of whom had had any intervention. He wrote early in the history of NLD, when little was known, largely for other professionals. Many parents find his books depressing; NLD is not as gloomy as he makes it seem.

Understanding Nonverbal Learning Disabilities. Maggie Mamen provides a good and relatively recent book especially helpful for teachers and professionals. It introduces the idea of subtypes of NLD.

The Internet

There are a number of ways to interact through the internet:

- E-mailing lists
- Blogs
- Websites
- Social media, including Twitter, Facebook, Google+
- More specialized social media about specific subjects

An **e-mailing list** is a way for people with a common interest to communicate to each other. Rather than sending an email to one person, you send it to an entire group, and then the people in the group can read it and respond through email.

Two e-mailing groups devoted to NLD are:

NLD-in-common is for anyone interested in NLD. To subscribe, send a blank e-mail to NLD-in-common-subscribe@ yahoogroups.com or go to the Yahoo groups page on at www .yahoo.com/groups.

NLD-adult is only for adults with NLD and requires permission of the moderator to join.

These lists vary considerably, in several ways:

- Moderated vs. unmoderated
- Open vs. closed
- Replying etiquette

A moderated list has a moderator. This person runs the list and screens all messages. The advantage is you are saved the bother of getting (and deleting) spam and unwanted, totally off-topic mail. The disadvantage is there can be delays in getting mail posted, which can make it difficult for discussion.

An open list is open to anyone who wants to join; in a closed list, the list owner has to approve you, and the list may be open to only certain types of people.

Among the NLD-oriented lists, for example, NLD-in-common is open, whereas NLD-adult is closed. Thus, the first list is open to anyone who is interested in NLD, including not only people with NLD but parents of children with NLD, teachers of kids with NLD, people who have friends with NLD, and so on. NLD-adult is restricted to adults who themselves have NLD.

The advantages and disadvantages of open and closed lists depend on the subject matter. In the NLD lists, for example, the NLD-in-common discussions allow people with NLD to discuss topics with interested NTers. This is very valuable. NLD-adult, on the other hand, allows discussion that many be inappropriate for children.

Finally, mailing lists vary in whether the norm is to reply to just the person who sent the message, or to the whole list. The former keeps your inbox from overflowing, saving you the hassle of deleting mail you don't want. The latter allows for more general discussion. Whatever kind of list you join, it is a good idea to read the messages for a few days, and possibly to browse the archives if available, before jumping in. This can save a lot of embarrassment.

Blogs are places for discussion, gathering information, and finding resources. On personal blogs you can learn something about the blogger and share something about yourself. Unlike, say, chatting at a cocktail party, you can take your time figuring out what you want to say and how you want to say it. You can also alter it later.

WEBSITES
NLD on the Web: www.nldontheweb.org Devoted exclusively to NLD

LD Online: www.ldonline.org

Learning Disabilities Association: www.ldaamerica.org

Peter Flom: www.IAmLearningDisabled.com

NLD SCHOOL
I know of only one school devoted exclusively to NLD children: Franklin Academy, a college-preparatory boarding school in rural Connecticut. www.fa-ct.org

Bibliography

American Psychiatric Association. *Diagnostic and Statistical Manual of Mental Disorders, 5th Edition.* Arlington, VA: American Psychiatric Association, 2014.

Burger, N. R. *A Special Kind of Brain: Living with Nonverbal Learning Disability.* London, NJ: Jessica Kingsley, 2004.

Duke, M.P., Nowicki, S., Martin, E.A. *Teaching Your Child the Language of Social Success.* Atlanta: Peachtree Publishers, 1996.

Fast, Y. *Employment for People with Nonverbal Learning Disabilities and Asperger's Syndrome: Stories and Strategies.* London, NJ: Jessica Kingsley, 2004.

Howard, V.F, Williams, B.F., Lepper, C.E. *Very Young Children with Special Needs: A Foundation for Educators, Families, and Service Providers (4th Edition).* Boston: Pearson, 2009.

Kranowitz, C. *The Out of Sync Child.* New York: Penguin, 2006.

Kutscher, M. *Kids in the Syndrome Mix.* London, NJ: Jessica Kingsley, 2005.

Lavoie, R. *It's So Much Work to Be Your Friend.* New York: Touchstone, 2005.

Mamen, M. *Understanding Nonverbal Learning Disabilities.* London, NJ: Jessica Kingsley, 2005.

Nowicki, S., Duke, M. P. *Helping the Child Who Doesn't Fit In.* Atlanta: Peachtree Publishers, 1992.

Palombo, J. *Nonverbal Learning Disability: A Clinical Perspective.* New York: WW Norton, 2006.

Rourke, B. *Syndrome of Nonverbal Learning Disorder.* New York: Guilford Press, 1995.

Stewart, K. *Helping a Child with a Nonverbal Learning Disability.* Oakland, CA: New Harbinger Publications, 2007.

Thompson, S. *The Source for Nonverbal Learning Disabilities.* East Moline, IL: Linguisystems Inc., 1997.

Whitney, R. V. *Bridging the Gap: Raising a Child with Nonverbal Learning Disorder.* New York: Perigee, 2002.